Boyd gets to the heart of daily issues we all may face. Allow his transformational writing to enhance your daily walk with Jesus. I know it has mine!

David O. Martin, senior pastor, Mount Vernon Baptist Church, Albertville, Alabama

There are few people in the world who understand love and comfort with the clarity and purity of Boyd Bailey.

Bill Chapman, founder, camphighland.com

Perfect for anyone who needs a verbal hug, a shout of hope, or guidance on what the Bible says about the daily issues we experience.

Angie Jenkins, hospitality extraordinaire, National Christian Foundation

A Little Book of Comfort provided me with powerful wisdom, inspiration, and reassurance of the love and provision of God in all situations. Simply put, God's got it! In this book, Boyd helps us to more deeply believe, trust, and live in that truth!

Bob Lewis, founder, Lewis Leadership

Nuggets of comforting, yet thought provoking meditations to be prayed over, given away to others, or simply applied to living biblically. Thank you, Boyd, for a book that surprised, encouraged, and challenged me in fresh new ways.

Ida Morris Bell

Boyd Bailey has a real and practical grasp of Scripture. I always feel like Boyd is sitting with me and sharing his heart of joy and comfort. His words are a gift to the heart!

Betsy Chapman, Delta flight attendant

A daily "shot in the arm" of our gracious heavenly Father's unchanging truth, encouragement, and comfort to combat the lies, discouragement, and despair instigated and fueled by the world, the flesh, and the devil.

Alison Ibsen, horse whisperer

Boyd Bailey has provided an outstanding resource to encourage us as we walk through the valleys of life. We've all been there. And we all need the Lord's comfort.

Jeremy Morton, copastor,
First Baptist, Woodstock, Georgia

Boyd Bailey is an exceptional human being. Boyd has bravely walked his own journey of pain and discovered the sweetness of resting in his heavenly Father's love and comfort. Out of an overflow of God's comfort, he beautifully shares that comfort with others through his writings.

Jodi Ward, licensed professional counselor

This "little" book not only provides comfort, it shares the truth of God's Word and the reality of His love in the daily living of our lives.

Kelly Shepherd, National Christian Foundation

These messages of hope, mercy, love, comfort, humility, praise, and joy prepare my heart and mind for the day ahead. The Holy Spirit continually uses Boyd to hit the nail right on the head for what my heart needs to hear that day.

Christa Hurley, business owner

This book is an absolute gem! As a psychologist, I deal with hurting people on a daily basis, and I gleaned several fresh insights into the role of comfort that will help me to better love, serve, and counsel others.

Andy Ward, Ph.D., senior psychologist,
Ward Psychological Group, LLC

A Little Book of Comfort shares Jesus Christ's extravagant love for His children as the God of comfort. It continually reminds us to let God be God and be set free.

Anne Metz, charity research specialist,
National Christian Foundation

Boyd teaches us how to grow strong during adversity by leading us to God's words, where we find encouragement during times of despair and hope where there is darkness. This book is truly a gift that will renew your spirit.

Stan and Amy Reiff,
Partner Professional Practice Leader—Consulting

Boyd Bailey uses his amazing gift of scriptural discernment to lift us with the rich, truthful wisdom of God's Word. This marvelous little book will encourage you daily with God's big, loving care!

Deborah Ochs, Witchita, Kansas

This book encourages us to fully enjoy life but also to face reality, find safety in God, and begin to trust God and others around us with the hard stuff. Boyd reminds us through stories, inspiration, and scriptures to know and see how God's love is so much bigger than any hurt and any work we can do on our own.

Alanna Linden, SVP of network relations for National Christian Foundation

LITTLE

BOOK

COMFORT

BOYD AND RITA BAILEY

HARVEST HOUSE PUBLISHERS
EUGENE, OREGON

TWO MINUTES IN THE BIBLE is a trademark of Boyd Bailey. Harvest House Publishers, Inc., is the exclusive licensee of the trademark TWO MINUTES IN THE BIBLE.

Cover photo © suteishi / Getty Images

Cover by Bryce Williamson

A Little Book of Comfort
Copyright © 2018 by Boyd Bailey and Rita Bailey
Published by Harvest House Publishers
Eugene, Oregon 97408
www.harvesthousepublishers.com

ISBN 978-0-7369-7246-8 (pbk.)
ISBN 978-0-7369-7259-8 (eBook)

Library of Congress Cataloging-in-Publication Data is on file at the Library of Congress, Washington, DC.

Printed in the United States of America

18 19 20 21 22 23 24 25 26 / VP-Am / 10 9 8 7 6 5 4 3 2 1

To
James and Jean Isbill,
Jack and Geri McEntee,
Karen Melby,
and
Stan and Amy Reiff—
who all know Christ in the
fellowship of His sufferings.

Introduction

Additional pain may be necessary to
bring relief to our current pain.

Lily, our eight-year-old granddaughter, writhed in pain. Tears flowed as she frantically sought relief from an intrusive, needle-sized splinter. With an ambush-like attack, the nemesis had invaded the soft, tender area of her palm just below the thumb. Her mom comforted her—a personified God hug—and calmly and lovingly assured her firstborn all would be okay while also gingerly explaining how extraction brings relief, but only after additional pain.

Childhood does not often have a context for how to process pain. The thought of someone digging into her sensitive skin caused our precious baby to howl in fear, and tears flooded like a raging river after a heavy rain. Aunts, uncles, grandparents all stood around, sympathetic but feeling helpless.

Pain hurts.

How many of us have splinters embedded in our souls? Your hurt may be buried deep in the recesses of your memories, but on occasion it raises its ugly head because you discover it was buried alive. Your pain was forgotten through denial, but ongoing forgiveness in the power of the Spirit is the only remedy to remove the pain that past sins inflicted on your heart. You may never hear the words, "Will you forgive me?" but you can still forgive and, by God's grace, not be controlled by someone else's past shaming.

Be kind and compassionate to one another, forgiving each other, just as in Christ God forgave you (Ephesians 4:32).

Like a physical wound, a festering emotional hurt lingers with infection just below the surface: puffy, red, and swollen, intently waiting for love's lance to bring relief. The pus of pride infects the blood of our emotions as it flows through our hurting heart with venomous effect. Only the antivenin of humility can counteract pride's deadly outcome. Humility recognizes and admits that the struggle over unresolved conflict corrodes relationships and clouds our judgment. Only when we go to our offender or the one we have offended and seek reconciliation can we clear our consciences.

If you are offering your gift at the altar and there remember that your brother or sister has something against you, leave your gift there in front of the altar. First go and be reconciled to them; then come and offer your gift (Matthew 5:23-24).

Or maybe your wound is fresh. If so, take courage and forgive fast so the hurt doesn't fester and lie dormant in resentment, ready to attack with you unaware. When you are hurt or offended, the amount of time it takes you to thank God and forgive is an indicator of how close your walk is with Christ.

Some people die in bitterness. For others, it takes years, months, weeks, or days. For the more mature in their faith, it takes hours; for saints, seconds; and for those who walk closest to Christ, thanksgiving and forgiveness are simultaneous to the offense. By God's grace, keep no record of wrongs and you will be free to love others as your heavenly Father loves you.

> *Love is patient, love is kind. It does not envy, it does not boast, it is not proud. It does not dishonor others, it is not self-seeking, it is not easily angered, it keeps no record of wrongs (1 Corinthians 13:4-5).*

I pray these 90 writings will help you, with the support of others and the Holy Spirit, process your daily pains in a way that repairs your soul. Learn to rest in your sweet Savior's care.

> *Come to me, all you who are weary and burdened, and I will give you rest. Take my yoke upon you and learn from me, for I am gentle and humble in heart, and you will find rest for your souls. For my yoke is easy and my burden is light (Matthew 11:28-30).*

A Fellow Struggler and Overcomer in Christ,
Boyd Bailey
Roswell, Georgia

Sorrow Removed

He will swallow up death forever.
The Sovereign LORD will wipe away the tears from all faces;
he will remove his people's disgrace from all the earth.
The LORD has spoken.

Isaiah 25:8

Sorrow is the fruit of sin in a fallen world at liberty to inflict pain. No one is immune to sorrow. Sorrow is created by sin, death, divorce, selfishness, poverty, rejection, loss, and fear. Sorrow is all around, and it circles its prey like vultures around a carcass, ready to pick away at the meat of your soul. Sorrow does not discriminate based on your race, gender, social class, or stage of life. It causes a weepy heart and a weary mind over a lifetime.

Your sorrow may be overwhelming to the point of anguish and despair. The hurt is about to drive you crazy, and you feel you can't handle it. You have lost perspective, God seems a million miles away, and your situation has gone from bad to worse. You have hit a brick wall, life seems to be crumbling around you, and you have nowhere to turn.

But there is a rescuer for your drowning soul.

Rescue me from the mire,
do not let me sink;

deliver me from those who hate me,
from the deep waters (Psalm 69:14).

Jesus will save you. Ask Him to dive in and rescue you from thrashing about in the deep waters of your sorrows. Sorrow is not foreign to Him; He was a man acquainted with grief, inflicted with multiple sorrows. He is a sympathetic Savior waiting to soothe your pain and gently wipe away your tears.

Take the medication of God's grace and administer larger doses in the beginning to stop the spread of sorrow's infection. He wants you to experience His abundant life in Christ, and He wipes away your tears not only in heaven, but on earth. Let God remove your points of sorrow one by one, as if they are trees downed by a storm's horrific winds. Sorrow is temporary with God; His joy is permanent.

He was despised and rejected by mankind,
a man of suffering, and familiar with pain
(Isaiah 53:3).

The Results of Worry

Can any one of you by worrying add
a single hour to your life?

Matthew 6:27

The results of worry aren't redeeming, productive, or helpful, and its ultimate sideways energy sidetracks us from our heavenly Father's loving comfort. Worry doesn't assist today, and it only complicates tomorrow. It's a dark alley in a loud, confused city. It's an untrodden trail off the beaten path of God's will. Worry has a way of putting a wrench into the works of Christ, and it's a subtle and not-so-subtle way to place our efforts ahead of God's.

Worry can become a self-fulfilling prophecy. We can work ourselves into a frantic state of self-reliance, so much so that we begin to believe and live out lies. We predict the worst-case scenario is imminent and then act in ways that move us in that direction. Worry leads to a victim mind-set. We simmer in pity, talking like a victim, and then we become a victim. Worry whispers questions like "What if you lose your job?" and "What if you have a disease?" and "What if he leaves you?"

Worry's results wreak havoc.

Let the peace of Christ rule in your hearts, since as members of one body you were called to peace. And be thankful (Colossians 3:15).

Praise the Lord for remedies to worry! Shifting our focus from self to our Savior is a foolproof way for faith to preempt false thinking. Self is like a jealous lover who wants to be the center of attention, but Christ alone deserves this highest status of affection. When our idols of security, money, control, and comfort bow to Jesus, worry runs away rejected. Worship embraces hope as courage for the heart, and courage and hope are fraternal twins that birth in us a living faith.

Furthermore, your humility in confessing your ongoing need for Christ leads to spiritual sustainability in Him. Healthy soul care requires you to invite your heavenly Father to care for your anxious heart and nervous emotions. Submission to our Sovereign God precludes a position for your pride to perch.

Yes, Jesus's spoken words in Scripture soothe your soul and bring peace to your war of worry. The result of trust is peace and calm.

> *Humble yourselves, therefore, under God's mighty hand, that he may lift you up in due time. Cast all your anxiety on him because he cares for you (1 Peter 5:6-7).*

Tears of Comfort

Jesus wept. Then the Jews said, "See how he loved him!"

John 11:35-36

A nonverbal language of love is communicated through compassionate tears because empathy engages the heart at levels that verbal exchanges may not be able to penetrate.

When emotion responds to emotion, grieving souls sense they are cared for and understood. Tears quietly convey that I feel your pain—I hurt because you hurt.

Comfort is the first step in seeking to serve another's pain, so refrain from truth-telling until the heart receives proper care. Fear and anger must be flushed from a hurting heart before facts can be appropriately comprehended and applied to the situation. People trust and receive from a context of love and acceptance, and tears become a conduit for Christ's care.

This is what the LORD, the God of your father
David, says: I have heard your prayer and seen
your tears; I will heal you (2 Kings 20:5).

Desperation feeds at the table of aloneness. But security and peace preoccupy the person comforted by a community, so we mourn with those who mourn so they are not alone. Starting with a patient spouse or friend, the mourning spills over to sincere souls who believe in Jesus to bring wholeness and healing. Tears shed in love terminate isolation and invite intimacy.

Does your husband, wife, or child need a response of compassion, rather than a reaction of passion? Does your team at work need you first to listen and understand, instead of feeling they must always meet an automatic demand based on your own agenda? Yes, truth sets us free, but the mind comprehends after the heart has been heard. Tears prepare the way for truth's arrival.

How is *your* heart? Do you have a safe environment to lay bare your soul? Self-reliance and self-condemnation are obstacles to intimacy with your heavenly Father and with those who love you the most. Dismiss driven discipline; instead, practice vulnerable dependency. Replace shame with security in your Savior and trusting transparency with a caring community. Your tears open your heart to emotional and spiritual healing, so free your soul to speak with moist eyes to your Master, Jesus, as He lovingly weeps with you.

I saw the tears of the oppressed—and they
have no comforter (Ecclesiastes 4:1).

> Who can I weep with and comfort in Christ? What in my heart needs healing comfort?

Responding to Senseless Violence

Why should my face not look sad when the city
where my ancestors are buried lies in ruins, and
its gates have been destroyed by fire?

Nehemiah 2:3

I sit here stunned, deeply saddened by the senseless violence of an evil man who massacred my fellow human beings at an outdoor concert. Some who died knew the Lord, and others did not, but all met their Maker on the most unexpected day. My heart quivers and quails at the thought of the defenseless and innocent being riddled by bullets. My anger, grief, and loss are distant compared to that of the families and friends the victims left behind. I weep. I pray. I hug my family. But what else is God calling me to do?

Nehemiah came face-to-face with the intense suffering of families and friends in his homeland. One of his brothers had just informed him of the chaotic and defenseless condition of the Jewish exiles who had returned to Jerusalem, only to find it in ruins. No security. No leadership. No hope. Only the prospect of fear and famine. Nehemiah lived in ease, peace, and affluence, but his countryman battled affliction, poverty, and sorrow. The innocents' exposure to evil and injustice moved Nehemiah to return to his people and provide a hopeful, practical plan.

He will rescue them from oppression and violence,
for precious is their blood in his sight (Psalm 72:14).

How can we help? God may call us to serve those far away who were struck down by senseless violence—certainly family and friends. Mourning, comfort, counseling, and Christ's gospel are much needed now and for years to come. And for all of us, we can be more circumspect about how to help our community prevent sinful atrocities or to help bring healing to those suffering from sinful actions—their own or another's. Someone's sadness is our opportunity to offer gladness.

Maybe your role becomes like that of the king who resourced Nehemiah to carry out his cause for justice and reinventing his community. Your generous investment of time, expertise, and money can make a difference in your world. Invest in mentoring to keep boys and girls from becoming another statistic of broken men and women. Initiate a movement of prayer in your church, asking the Holy Spirit to breathe on believers with a fresh fire of faith and repentance. The cross was sad, senseless violence that became God's plan of salvation—and it still is today!

Having disarmed the powers and authorities, [Jesus] made a public spectacle of them, triumphing over them by the cross (Colossians 2:15).

How can I give, serve, and pray for those who are victims of violence?

A God Hug

Shout for joy, you heavens;
rejoice, you earth;
burst into song, you mountains!
For the LORD comforts his people
and will have compassion on his afflicted ones.

Isaiah 49:13

A God hug is a timely gift. His hugs soothe, comfort, and calm. He is never late in offering His affection or too busy to stand still and embrace His human creation. The Spirit gently caresses burdened shoulders and rubs out raw pain in the backs of believers. His compassion has never failed; His mercy is fresh every day. Like a cool cream alleviates an itchy rash, so His balm of grace relieves a rash of worries. A God hug holds on tight until healing occurs.

Furthermore, a God hug does not happen on the run, but while we stand still. "Slow down, My child," He says. "Hush, I have this. Be still. Let Me hold you. Rest in My arms." So we learn to stay stationary by faith and trust the right activities will get done in the right time. When we schedule appointments to be loved by the Lord, we receive strength for the journey. Otherwise, we exhaust our ability to encourage without the infusion of Christ's courage. His hugs hearten.

*Praise be to the God and Father of our Lord Jesus
Christ, the Father of compassion and the God of all
comfort, who comforts us in all our troubles, so that we
can comfort those in any trouble with the comfort we
ourselves receive from God (2 Corinthians 1:3-4).*

Affection from the Almighty makes us attractive to those who need our compassion and care, and our hugs from Jesus compel us to hug others with unconditional love. For example, we may receive an unexpected financial blessing, so we are able to show generosity to another's cash challenge. An insight from Scripture or a kind word from a friend could be passed on to someone who needs our encouragement. God comforts us, so we can comfort others.

Shout for joy in praise to your Creator for His comfort and compassion. Brag on His name and extol Him for His divine affection. Like the father of the prodigal son who came home, your Father in heaven can't wait to embrace you in your shame, stress, or success. He runs to greet you with warm acceptance, so throw yourself into His arms. Cast your cares on Christ and abandon your life to the Lord. Yes, enjoy His sweet embrace!

*I will turn their mourning into gladness;
I will give them comfort and joy instead
of sorrow (Jeremiah 31:13).*

The Fruit of Pain

Someone may be chastened on a bed of pain
with constant distress in their bones,
so that their body finds food repulsive
and their soul loathes the choicest meal...
Let their flesh be renewed like a child's.

Job 33:19-20,25

A variety of spiritual fruit can be produced out of pain. One is the clear understanding of what breaks the heart of God, because sin may surface through the sifting of suffering that invites genuine contrition, confession, and repentance. The pain can be a symptom of a wound either self-inflicted or inflicted from an unfair situation or an insensitive person, but whether sin has entered the heart from the inside or out, it requires attention. Without it, the soul will erode. Distress that draws us to God instead purifies our hearts.

Another spiritual fruit from pain is instruction from the Lord. Pain is an opportunity for God to instruct His children in a better way. A human being on his back is much more teachable than an individual running to and fro in frantic activity. We look up to heaven when we lie down faceup, leveled by the forces of physical and/or emotional upheaval. Yes, our loving heavenly Father whispers intimate instruction to His loved ones who listen to His voice.

Pain gives insight into God.

[Jesus said to His disciples,] "My soul is overwhelmed
with sorrow to the point of death. Stay here and
keep watch with me" (Matthew 26:38).

Our heavenly Father's comfort is yet another outcome of suffering under the yoke of pain. As we cry out
in desperate dependence on Him, He assures us of His
presence—perhaps through our Savior's silent reassurance:
His speaking through another sincere saint, His calming us
with a change in circumstance, or His soothing our soul
with Scripture. The Lord is not limited in His long arm of
care and comfort. Our pain is His opportunity to apply His
healing balm of love.

See pain as a pass-through for the grace of God in your
life. Your challenges become a conduit to care for other hurting hearts. Your energy is not consumed by your cares alone,
but out of the depths of personal hurt you are able to bring
the Spirit of your empathizing Savior, Jesus, to others. You
consume the fruit of pain with your hungry heart, and your
fruitful spirit feeds others who feel out of favor with God.

Enjoy Christ's sweet comfort, and comfort other hurting hearts.

He will comfort us in the labor and painful
toil of our hands caused by the ground the
LORD has cursed (Genesis 5:29).

Obey When Afraid

"Come," [Jesus] said. Then Peter got down out of the
boat, walked on the water and came toward Jesus.

Matthew 14:29

Sometimes Jesus sends us ahead in our boat of faith while
He prays for us from a distance. We feel alone at times
because He is not physically beside us to provide reassurance
that we are on the right course. Then when global uncertainty or storms of sickness strike our core belief, we become
fearful. In our crisis of faith, we can either get out of our boat
of fear and walk on the water toward Jesus or sink in unbelief.

Are you waiting to launch out in faith? Are you in the
middle of a storm anticipating His reassurance any minute? Or has He asked you to get out of the boat for a major
faith-stretching goal? Wherever you are in your continuum
of faith in Christ, trust Him in the transition. If you are on
the shore, get in the boat of belief. If you are in the middle
of one of life's fearful storms, look for Christ coming toward
you. If He is asking you to get out of the boat and walk on
water, trust Him.

[We must fix] our eyes on Jesus, the pioneer and
perfecter of faith. For the joy set before him he endured
the cross, scorning its shame, and sat down at the
right hand of the throne of God (Hebrews 12:2).

What seems unnatural or impossible to you may be reasonable to Him. Obedience is not a blind leap of faith, for you are fixing your eyes on Jesus. Do not look to the left at the storm, to the right at the still shore, or down at the uncertain water. Look straight ahead into the confident eyes of Christ. Watch Him as you walk on water in faith.

We walk on water not to be seen but to see Him. A depth of trust and love for the Lord comes only from walking toward Him with virgin legs. Like a child learning to walk looks toward the outstretched arms of his loving parent, so we wobble toward our smiling Savior. Go with God and experience great gain, or stay where you are and suffer great loss. Move out of your comfort zone so Christ can be your sole comfort.

Stay in the boat and see your limited work, or walk on water and see His unlimited work.

Now to him who is able to do immeasurably more than all we ask or imagine, according to his power that is at work within us (Ephesians 3:20).

Where is the Lord asking me to get out of my comfort zone and go with Him?

Stilled and Quieted

I have calmed and quieted myself,
I am like a weaned child with its mother;
like a weaned child I am content.

Psalm 131:2

The raging waves of the world's worries crash against the shore of our souls. At work it may be missed deadlines or mismanagement of money. At home it may be miscommunication or a "monster" of a child. At school it may be the misconduct of others or the misfortune of feeling alone. Life is loud, and sometimes its deafening tones tune out our trust in God.

Only in silence can our souls be resuscitated by our Savior, Jesus, who works wonders when we wait before Him. We are clamorous without Christ, but by grace our souls are subdued and soothed. Calm and contentment come forth by faith when we are stilled and quieted before Christ.

One example is the emotional word picture of parental love.

As a mother comforts her child,
so will I comfort you;
and you will be comforted over Jerusalem (Isaiah 66:13).

A mother is a comfort to her weaned child, even though she has denied that child a comfort previously known. As you linger quietly with the Lord in anticipation, what He gives you may not be what you want but what you need. You may want to leave, but He knows you need to stay. You may want to start a ministry, but He knows you need to run a business. You may want to marry, but He knows you need to mature more in your faith and grow more stable in your finances. You may want to get, but He knows you need to give.

You may want a promotion, but He knows you need to learn faithfulness and contentment where you currently work. The Holy Spirit may be weaning you off someone or something so you will want and need only Him.

So still and quiet your soul by inviting your heavenly Father's warm embrace. You can sleep well when He holds you. By God's grace, remain childlike in your faith and character. Keep your heart humble and honest under heaven's hope. Like a child looks to his mother for comfort and security, look to your Savior, Jesus, for His quiet confidence and strength.

A heart kept by Christ lives for Christ. Settle your soul in stillness and solitude with Jesus.

> *[Jesus] said, "Truly I tell you, unless you change*
> *and become like little children, you will never*
> *enter the kingdom of heaven" (Matthew 18:3).*

What routines can I integrate into my daily life so I can be still and quiet before Christ?

Fear Represses Faith

Many even among the leaders believed in
him. But because of the Pharisees they would
not openly acknowledge their faith for fear they
would be put out of the synagogue; for they loved
human praise more than praise from God.

John 12:42-43

Fear represses faith and restrains its recognition. It holds back the boldness to believe because fear is no friend of faith. Fear mistakenly believes it can coddle cunning people while at the same time claim Christ. This is a contradiction that does not stand up under the scrutiny of your Savior because Jesus requires unconditional commitment and unwavering loyalty. Faith is not motivated by fear of people, but by love of God, and it does not seek to integrate other belief systems into Christianity. Total trust embraces Jesus, and Jesus alone.

Believers who acknowledge—or profess—their faith in Christ are set free from fear because confession is freeing while repression is constraining. You may currently be flailing away on the battlefield of fear. You fear how others may perceive you if they know you fear God. They may label you as weird, narrow-minded, or judgmental, but acknowledgment of Christ risks being misunderstood for the sake of the Lord. It values praise from God over praise from humans. Yes, public profession of your faith may cost you. Leaders especially have a lot to lose by laying their beliefs on the line.

> *Saul replied, "I have sinned. But please honor*
> *me before the elders of my people and before*
> *Israel; come back with me, so that I may worship*
> *the LORD your God" (1 Samuel 15:30).*

How can you be a quiet Christian? Where are the leaders who will live by principle even when it may mean losing power? Don't use your faith just to get a following, and don't compromise your convictions just to please a group that refuses to respect your values. Fear-based decision-making has no place in the lives of Christ's disciples. Do the right thing, even though it may cost you votes, a job, a raise, a promotion, praise, or opportunities. Do not fear—obey Christ.

When you give up something because of principle, you gain His praise. When fear becomes your fortress, you fight a losing battle, for fear is indefensible. You cannot do enough to defend its exposed flank; therefore, fight fear with a consistent and compassionate public acknowledgment of Christ. Trust God to use your profession for His cause and glory.

Public acknowledgment of Christ gives confidence and calm, and fear melts under the heat of that profession.

*Offer to God a sacrifice of praise—the fruit of lips
that openly profess his name (Hebrews 13:15).*

> What fear has neutralized my faith and caused me
> unnecessary worry and stress?

Happiness in Grief

Blessed are those who mourn, for they will be comforted.

Matthew 5:4

Life is a series of gains and losses. We gain friends, and we lose friends. We gain confidence, and we lose confidence. We gain money, and we lose money. We gain a position, and we lose a position. We gain weight, and we lose weight. We gain perspective, and we lose perspective. Many times during the transition between our gain and our loss, we grieve, or grief follows loss. But it's in our grieving that God gets our attention.

Who or what do you miss? A loved one who graduated to heaven, a career you enjoyed, or children who have left the nest and started their own families? Perhaps your heart still aches from time to time. Anger may well up occasionally, or your mind may play tricks on you with what-if scenarios, causing you to doubt your decisions. In this contemplative process, however, we learn to listen to the Lord—to trust Him and be loved by Him.

Job experienced the Lord in his loss: "The lowly he sets on high, and those who mourn are lifted to safety" (Job 5:11).

You can experience comfort from Christ during your grief from a loss. We all live in a house that contains rooms of mourning. We avoid these areas, but eventually we must visit them. And we learn that the greater the grief, the greater the potential for gladness. God's goodness becomes the glue for our fractured faith.

Spiritual grief comes when we are separated from God by our sin, and we mourn over our broken fellowship. Spiritual mourners lament when their sin isolates them from intimacy with Christ, but a godly sorrow is sensitive to sin and quick to repent. So do not linger long in grief over letting down the Lord—freely receive His forgiveness.

Last, look for those around you who silently suffer or who, unbeknownst to you, may be grieving. Followers of Jesus empathize by mourning with those who mourn. Take the time to come alongside them and offer care, comfort, and Christ. Weep with those who weep while the Lord's love wipes away their tears.

Jesus ministered to the grieving while on earth, and He still comforts and makes hearts happy through the Holy Spirit.

The Comforter, which is the Holy Ghost, whom the Father will send in my name, he shall teach you all things, and bring all things to your remembrance, whatsoever I have said unto you (John 14:26 KJV).

Is Christ my comfort during times of grief? Who is someone I can comfort who is grieving a loss?

Love Always Trusts

[Love] always protects, always trusts,
always hopes, always perseveres.

1 Corinthians 13:7

Love always trusts, for trust is a staple of love. If you are always suspicious and uncertain, love is lacking. Love thrives in an environment of trust but shrivels in a spirit of distrust. To love without trust is difficult, for trust is a lubricant for love. Trust calls out love like an engagement invitation; it's essential for a love relationship to take root and flourish. Look for the best in someone else and trust them, even though they may not have been trustworthy in the past. Love is all about second chances.

Of course, you must be a responsible steward of money and time, so don't blindly trust everything everyone tells you. Have a policy of "trust and verify." On the other hand, love does not write someone off when they fail to meet expectations or experience failure. Love picks them up and says, "I will trust you again. I have not given up on you. You are on the team. You are a child of God, and you deserve another opportunity to succeed."

> *Whoever lives in love lives in God, and*
> *God in them (1 John 4:16).*

Love always trusts, and this is especially true with Almighty God. Love trusts God, for His track record is without blemish. If you love Him, you will trust Him. Your affection and love are meant to originate in heaven, not on earth. Love leans on and listens to the Lord because it trusts Him, so the goal is to fall more deeply in love with God. Go deeper with God, and you will become more and more infatuated with Him and His ways.

John explains it well: "We know and rely on the love God has for us. God is love" (1 John 4:16).

God is your lover. He is a lover of your mind, soul, body, and emotions. You can trust Him to love you authentically and unconditionally. He has no inhibitions in His intimate love for you. Your trust in God accelerates in direct proportion to your intimacy with Jesus. Love the Lord long and hard. Hug heaven often, and watch your trust increase.

Let the morning bring me word of your unfailing love,
for I have put my trust in you.
Show me the way I should go,
for to you I entrust my life (Psalm 143:8).

With what concern do I need to trust Christ and His love to take care of, in His timing?

Suffering from a Redefinition of Marriage

In the image of God he created them; male and
female he created them. God blessed them
and said to them, "Be fruitful and increase in
number; fill the earth and subdue it."

Genesis 1:27-28

I feel disappointed, angry, and yet hopeful by the debate in our country over the definition of marriage. I feel disappointed in Christian marriages (mine included) for not being a better example of a Christ-honoring relationship in the last 40 years. I feel angry with most of our citizens (many who are Christians) who are repurposing God's purpose for marriage. I feel hopeful for the opportunity Jesus-followers have to love like Jesus in the middle of opposition to His moral code while living what we believe by modeling grace-filled marriages that men and women would aspire to.

Our heavenly Father's heart of love desires to bless male and female—both created in His image. However, if we redefine marriage as other than one woman and one man in holy matrimony, we create an unholy ritual expedient for selfish, personal gain. Marriage without the distinctive of one male and one female is not marriage at all. Call it a civil union approved by the state, but do not call it a marriage blessed by Almighty God. Marriage is a covenant before God, between a man and a woman. The marriage of a man and woman is built on the image of our holy God.

What therefore God has joined together, let not man put asunder (separate) (Matthew 19:6 AMPC).

Marriage defined as the union of a man and a woman was never in question for our Lord. He attended a wedding and blessed it with His presence and His present of abundant wine. Marriage for Jesus was the timeless, divinely ordained institution of a man and woman exclusively committed to each other for a lifetime of growing deeper in love with each other. Just as we are faithful to Christ throughout our lives, we seek to be faithful to our husband or wife. Marriage is an opportunity for a man and woman to become one in Christ's love. Marriage is a journey with Jesus.

Most of all, in the middle of the marriage debate, let's model our marriages under Christ's authority—full of humility and love. Let's ask God's mercy and forgiveness for misrepresenting His marriage plan. Let's hope and pray God's marriage purpose becomes so real in our marriages that it is held and revered as the standard for all marriages to become image bearers of God.

Let us rejoice and be glad
and give him glory!
For the wedding of the Lamb has come,
and his bride has made herself ready (Revelation 19:7).

Emotional Satisfaction

The LORD will guide you always;
he will satisfy your needs in a sun-scorched land
and will strengthen your frame.
You will be like a well-watered garden.

Isaiah 58:11

Emotional satisfaction comes from Christ—from a focus on His eternal satisfaction. My feelings of fulfillment will not rise any higher than my faith in Jesus to meet my every need. Of course, close confidants can provide emotional needs like love, laughter, security, and companionship.

But unless the backdrop of my emotional desires is based on my belief in and dependence on God, I will never be satisfied. Contentment is in Christ alone—period.

Isaiah illustrates this with the compelling imagery of a life suffering a spiritual drought that can be irrigated only by the love of God. Sin and secular society scorch our souls with their dry and brittle influences, but the living water of Jesus brings life and longing for the Lord to quench our thirsty hearts. Imagine a luscious, green garden laden with fruits and vegetables—likewise, we feast on the fruit of soul satisfaction. Emotional fullness from our heavenly Father never stops flowing—never. The spigot of our Savior's love is always turned on by faith in His persistent provision.

Satisfy us in the morning with your unfailing love, that we may sing for joy and be glad all our days (Psalm 90:14).

Do you feel dissatisfied and discontent? A pride in what you have and an ego demanding what you want can keep you from enjoying what the Lord has already given you in Jesus. A daily eulogy spoken over the world's dead idols of affection tries to speak life into what only the Lord's unfailing love can provide you: peace and joy! Emotional satisfaction can be aloof and elusive, but in Christ it is close by and obtainable. Set the focus of your affections above in heaven, not below on earth. Make faith the queen bee of your hive of life, and the emotional worker bees will follow. Feelings that follow faith create emotional health and satisfaction.

Do not be afraid to share your fears with friends and family who love you, because emotional vulnerability can lead to emotional healing and wholeness. An awakened and open soul has much more capacity to love and be loved. Emotional satisfaction from secular remedies is hollow, but emotional satisfaction from spiritual solutions—like worship—results in a grateful life.

The Lord is your guide into your feelings. The Creator of your emotions understands and calms your fears. Seek your Savior, Jesus, to satisfy your emotional needs.

May your unfailing love be my comfort (Psalm 119:76).

> Whom can I trust to share what I feel, to receive their comfort and prayers?

Heartsick

Have compassion on me, LORD, for I am weak.
Heal me, LORD, for my bones are in agony.
I am sick at heart.
How long, O LORD, until you restore me?
Return, O LORD, and rescue me.
Save me because of your unfailing love.

Psalm 6:2-4 NLT

The human heart is fragile and can easily fracture under the weight of disappointment and fear. Questions lurk in the background, waiting to assault someone's confidence: Am I good enough? Am I attractive enough? Am I smart enough? Am I wealthy enough? Am I secure enough? Am I mature enough? Outside of Christ, we can never feel we are enough.

We struggle with these insecurities when we suffer rejection from those we thought loved and accepted us. Our trust is tortured when we experience severe relational letdown. We ask, "Wasn't this the one I was supposed to marry?" Or "Wasn't I in line for the promotion, but my colleague was rewarded instead of me?" "Why do we have to sell our dream home after all these years of hard work?" Heartsickness depletes our energy.

Hope deferred makes the heart sick, but a
longing fulfilled is a tree of life
(Proverbs 13:12).

Emotional and spiritual weakness dim the rays of hope that once lit our path. But in our despair, we can't forget that Jesus is there. The Lord's compassion does not fail. It does not fail in its appearance, and it does not fail in its application. Like a massage to a strained muscle, a warm whirlpool to a twisted ankle, or a protective splint to a broken bone, God brings comfort and healing to a suffocating soul. He restores hope to the uttermost.

Is your faith moody and unpredictable? Are you hurting? If so, seek out the healing hand of your heavenly Father. Let go of the pain of rejection and forgive those who turned their backs on you. Turn your eyes to Jesus and look to His healing hand. Your sick heart needs the reassuring serum from your empathizing Savior, the hope that heals the heart.

Moreover, care for those who feel crushed under their own circumstances. Be patient with their complaints; they need the support of your comfort and concern. As from the trauma of a car accident, they may be scared and shaken. Pray with and for them to trust God and to place their hurting heart in His hands.

Indeed, be a spiritual cardiologist for Christ.

Light in a messenger's eyes brings joy to the heart, and good news gives health to the bones (Proverbs 15:30).

How can I apply hope in the Lord to my sick heart?
Whose heart can I comfort through prayer?

Overcome by Fear

Then all the people of the region of the Gerasenes asked Jesus to leave them, because they were overcome with fear. So he got into the boat and left.

Luke 8:37

Fear drives out faith, and overwhelming fear withdraws faith's invitation to come to Jesus. Why? Because Jesus is a gentleman. He does not tarry where He is not trusted or wanted, and He does not negotiate to be needed. Yes, faith is exhausted in the face of overwhelming fear, and this is especially true when your chronic fear relates to money. Money, more than almost anything, can make you myopic to faith in God.

You can get so consumed by the crises of current financial affairs that you forget your anchor in Almighty God. A preoccupation with money is a symptom of something else beneath the surface. Money is not the answer, however, because Jesus is the dependable security you desire. Do not dismiss prayer and patience just because you feel out of control. This is when you are tempted to behave like an atheist. You say you believe in God, and that He is in control and you trust Him, but your behavior betrays your beliefs. You act like an unbeliever when your actions marginalize your Master.

Be still, and know that I am God (Psalm 46:10).

Fear keeps you looking over your shoulder in doubt, but all the while your Savior is right beside you, waiting to be your calming force. Take the time to tarry in trust with the One who is totally trustworthy. Do not drive Him away in denial. Rise up from under the load of your languishing condition and go to Christ for perspective and patience.

Don't panic, but exorcise your overwhelming fear by faith. Surrender to your Savior, Jesus.

Now is your opportunity to stand firm and courageous in Christ. Talk is easy, but your walk with Him is what matters. He desires an authentic and teachable heart. He can do this for you by faith, so let these uncertain times embolden you and strengthen your beliefs. Go deeper with Jesus during desperate days. Do not run Him off, for He will remain only where He is wanted. He is a gentleman waiting for your invitation to stay.

The LORD is my light and my salvation—
whom shall I fear? (Psalm 27:1).

What financial concern do I need to entrust to the Lord, standing firm by faith in Jesus?

No Longer a Slave to Fear

The Spirit you received does not make you slaves,
so that you live in fear again; rather, the Spirit
you received brought about your adoption to
sonship. And by him we cry, "Abba, Father."

Romans 8:15

Fear is a cruel master. Like a bad dream, fear imagines scary situations that will never take place. The fears in my mind seem so real that I stress—even obsess—over them. Recently, I became fearful of a worst-case scenario at work. I lost confidence and sleep. Finally, somewhat perturbed, I began to quietly reflect and remember how God is writing my story. In His script, His perfect love casts out my phobias. I am not a slave to fear, but to my Savior, Jesus.

The Lord adopted us as His daughters and sons, and the Spirit gives us life to live for Christ. In His power we can produce positive and lasting results. The Spirit allows us to put to death the deeds of the flesh (Romans 6:12-17) that promote fear. As we yield to the Spirit, He uses us for His purposes. Similar to what a gifted teacher does, the Holy Spirit instructs us in truth to combat fearful lies. He leads us as adopted children.

Fear has no place for a child cared for by King Jesus!

Those who are led by the Spirit of God are the children of God (Romans 8:14).

What do you fear? Confronting a coworker? Confessing a hidden sin to your spouse? A new school? A new job? A new relationship? A new responsibility? A health issue or lack of finances? Whatever you fear, ask the Holy Spirit to lovingly convert your fears into faith. Trust that when you have done the right thing, it will be what's right for everyone involved. Do not dread someone or something you have no control over. Instead, trust the Spirit to accomplish the appropriate outcome. Faith hands over all control to Christ.

You have been released from the fetters of trepidation and freed to trust Jesus. Your ball and chain of dread have been removed by the grace of God. Once you cowered in a corner of shame, but now you have come clean and placed your confidence in Christ. Fear acts like a malaria-carrying mosquito, only to discover the blood of Christ in your spiritual veins. Your heavenly Father's perfect love has replaced your pesky fears.

Fear wants you back in bondage, but God's love sets you free. Cry "Abba, Father" and fear not!

*The Spirit himself testifies with our spirit that
we are God's children (Romans 8:16).*

Loved to Love

We love because he first loved us.

1 John 4:19

Almighty God loves with an incredible love. His love has no boundaries or bias; it is limitless in His grace. His love goes behind the Enemy's lines of deceit and rescues those lost in their loveless state of mind. Christ's love looks for the unloved and offers comfort, care, compassion, and forgiveness.

The love of God is not without benefits. Those cloaked in the love of Christ will have great boldness on the Day of Judgment—indeed, His great love covers all sin for those who have appropriated His salvation. Moreover, fear is cast out of the peace-loving presence of the Lord's love. Fear and love cannot coexist where the love of Jesus fills humble hearts.

There is no fear in love. But perfect love
drives out fear (1 John 4:18).

Do you rest in the love of the Lord? Or do you strive under the unnecessary pressure of believing you must prove you deserve to be loved? Daily doses of eternal love are a remedy to earthly love's limited effectiveness. No matter their sincerity, no one can replace the need for the love of Jesus to fill the soul. Receive first God's love, and then let others' love be a bonus.

Why does the Almighty love you with such abandonment? One reason is so you can be a catalyst for Christ's love. You have the inconceivable opportunity to love others on behalf of the Lord. While a friend or family member writhes in physical agony or emotional pain, you are an extension of God's eternal love on earth because you are extremely loved by God. You have His extra love to administer to another's loneliness and frantic fears.

Take time to regularly receive the love of Jesus into your life. Commune with Christ, the lover of your soul, and you will experience His peace and security. Your rested spirit is positioned to be a robust lover for another love-hungry heart. Enter into God's eternal love so you can deploy it on earth. The Lord loves on you, so you can love on others.

God is love. Whoever lives in love lives in
God, and God in them (1 John 4:16).

Have I experienced my heavenly Father's love?
Whom can I love on?

Reasons Not to Be Fearful

Do not fear, for I am with you;
do not be dismayed, for I am your God.
I will strengthen you and help you.

Isaiah 41:10

Fear is a persistent foe, and I am unable to live 100 percent fear free. I can rest in the Lord's reassurance one minute, and then the next minute fear can make payroll. God's peace floods my soul during an uplifting worship service on Sunday, but on Monday morning I can wake up worried about a circumstance or person out of my control. How can I move more toward a life of faith than a life riddled with fear? *Trust in the Lord* is the short answer. Here are reasons not to be fearful:

God's Got It—Whatever "It" Is

What does that mean…*God's got it*? *God's got it* means we don't have to bear our burdens alone. God's got our health issues, so we can rest in His wellness. God's got our financial challenges, so we can look to His abundant provision. God's got our prodigal's rogue relationships, so we can trust Him with our child's protection. God's got our family, finances, career, and health—as well as our morally deteriorated culture. Since the Lord is in control, we can let go.

> *The king's heart is like channels of water in*
> *the hand of the LORD; He turns it whichever*
> *way He wishes (Proverbs 21:1 AMP).*

The Holy Spirit is at work where we are not. In the same way God's Spirit was brooding over a yet-to-be creation, so He is still at work creating something out of nothing. So as we pray for lost souls to be saved, the Holy Spirit is at work softening sinful hearts and drawing the unsaved to Himself. As we wait on the Lord, the Holy Spirit is at work lubricating the door hinges of opportunity to swing open in His timing. We may not like an authority's decision, but we know the Spirit is at work to reveal His truth. We dismiss fearfulness by trusting God.

Jesus is a faithful friend. He sticks closest to us when we are emotionally far away from others. When we experience loss, Jesus is there to weep with us, comfort us, and give us hope through the grieving process. When we are forsaken by a friend, Jesus walks with us in acceptance as we bear our cross of rejection. When we don't feel loved, Jesus loves us with empathy and understanding. Jesus is always with us to calm our fears.

Have I not commanded you? Be strong and courageous. Do not be afraid (Joshua 1:9).

What do I need to give to God, trusting Him with the outcome?

Gratitude and Contentment

Give thanks in all circumstances; for this is God's will for you in Christ Jesus...I know what it is to be in need, and I know what it is to have plenty. I have learned the secret of being content in any and every situation, whether well fed or hungry, whether living in plenty or in want.

1 Thessalonians 5:18; Philippians 4:12

Gratitude and contentment go together like turkey and dressing. They feed each other, and both are fostered by faith. When I remember how God has so richly blessed me, I am overwhelmed by His generosity. For my salvation by His Son, Jesus, I am eternally grateful. For His gift of grace, I am grateful for its freedom. For His forgiveness, I am grateful for guilt-free living. For His love, I am grateful for the ability to love and be loved. For His holiness, I am grateful His character can be trusted and is transformational.

Stuff is secondary, while the blessings of faith, family, friends, and health grow our contentment. We may not have what we want or even deserve, but in Christ we have all that is necessary. So be humbly grateful to God, and contentment will increase its influence.

> *The fear of the LORD leads to life; then one rests content, untouched by trouble (Proverbs 19:23).*

Contentment is to rest in Christ, trusting He is in control. Circumstances, good or bad, are an opportunity for Him to show Himself faithful, so once you go to God in gratitude, you can live life in contentment knowing Christ is in control. Contentment is not passive and uninformed, but rather engaged and educated. It is not anxious. It replaces worry with work, self-pity with prayer, pride with humility, and grumbling with gratitude.

Your peace and stability are the fruit of contentment, which grows out of the ground of gratitude. Seed this soil in prayer, and you will see abundance abound. You can flourish in adversity because the Almighty has gone before you.

You can bridle wants during times of prosperity because gratitude to God and contentment in Christ govern your generosity. Thank God often, and trust Him to cultivate your contentment.

> *I can do all things through Christ who*
> *strengthens me (Philippians 4:13 NKJV).*

What are some reasons for my gratitude to God, and how can I express my contentment in Christ?

Ongoing Gratitude

> Whatever you do, whether in word or deed, do
> it all in the name of the Lord Jesus, giving
> thanks to God the Father through him.
>
> *Colossians 3:17*

It is God's will for us to give thanks in all circumstances. How can this be? In triumph and good things, yes, but am I to be grateful in defeat and bad things? Many times Christ's thoughts are counterintuitive to man's shallow assumptions. The Lord in His wonderful wisdom understands the advantage of thanksgiving in both prosperity and adversity.

Perhaps we experience the union of a child and spouse who love the Lord, and we rejoice in their marriage and give

God the glory. Conversely, we have the heartbreak of a child who cannot keep a marriage together, and it ends in divorce. In this dark day of disappointment, we still say to our Savior, "Thank You for working all things out for the good of those who love You." Thanksgiving governs our joy, peace, and contentment.

> *We know that in all things God works for the good of those who love him, who have been called according to his purpose (Romans 8:28).*

Gratitude is also first cousins with humility. It's out of the fertile soil of thanksgiving that humility can grow and flourish. Gratitude says, "Thank You, God, for giving me salvation in Jesus," while humility says, "I want to go deeper in my intimacy with Jesus." Gratitude says, "Friends are a gift from God," while humility says, "How can I serve my friends?"

> *I always thank my God as I remember you in my prayers, because I hear about your love for all his holy people and your faith in the Lord Jesus (Philemon 1:4-5).*

Furthermore, gratitude gives you the positive energy to engage life and live it to the fullest. Out of your thanksgiving, you can understand God's will and follow Jesus wholeheartedly. You can complain to Christ, just not about Christ. He wants more for you than you want for yourself, so be extremely grateful, ever rejoicing in Him.

*Do not be anxious about anything, but in every
situation, by prayer and petition, with thanksgiving,
present your requests to God (Philippians 4:6).*

How has the Lord blessed my life? How can I express
my gratitude to Him and others?

Path of Peace

The rising sun will come to us from heaven to shine
on those living in darkness and in the shadow of
death, to guide our feet into the path of peace.

Luke 1:78-79

Jesus, the Prince of Peace, was born on earth to provide for
His people a path of peace. The path is fraught with rocks,
steep hills, pelting rain, shades of night, and confusing cross-
roads. However, regardless of the resistance encountered on
the Lord's path, an inner peace is available to the sometimes
doubtful and weary traveler. Yes, the foundation of tranquil-
lity is trust in Christ. His light on life's path brings steps of
peace to faithful feet.

Are you stumbling through life in need of a Savior?
Or are your feet of faith planted on the solid ground of
salvation? Your uncertain feet can find confidence with

dependency on the Lord. Your soiled feet can be cleansed and refreshed by His forgiveness. Your tired feet can enjoy a comforting massage from your Master, Jesus. Your fast feet may need to slow down, and your slow feet may need to speed up. Ask God to guide your next wise step.

> *[Wisdom's] ways are pleasant ways, and all*
> *her paths are peace (Proverbs 3:17).*

Beams of light from your belief in God will show you the way. The dark world is scary and sometimes confusing, but the Light of the world illumines peace and clarity on your prayerful path. Like a flashlight, your faith burns bright. A shadow of death eventually eclipses us all, but those in Christ wake up to the brightness of His presence!

Choose the narrow, well-lit path of peace and avoid the wide, darkened path of turmoil. The route of the majority tends to major on the minors, but God's righteous remnant walk in His light of love with illuminating intimacy. Stay the course of your convictions, and your Savior, Jesus, will show you the way. He came to earth under a peaceful canopy of heaven's candles, and He will return in a blaze of blinding glory!

> *Glory to God in the highest heaven, and on*
> *earth peace to those on whom his favor rests*
> *(Luke 2:14).*

Worship God Through Your Pain

*Job got up and tore his robe and shaved his
head. Then he fell to the ground in worship.*

Job 1:20

Are you struggling to understand? Are you stuck in a state of anger? Have you lost something or someone precious? It may be the loss of your child's health or even the death of a child. A spouse may have gone to heaven or left you for someone else. Or your children are angry because they do not understand why you are divorcing. You are angry and hurt at your loss.

Is your heart hemorrhaging with pain and animosity? Everything you once held dear, that you took for granted, now is gone. You have no spouse, no children, no home, no job, and no money. This is a barren and lonely time for you; one is a lonely number. Where are you to turn when the bottom falls out? God seems detached, and heaven seems a trillion miles away.

*David got up from the ground. After he had washed, put
on lotions and changed his clothes, he went into the
house of the LORD and worshiped (2 Samuel 12:20).*

Worship the Lord in your pain and loss. Focusing on the greatness, holiness, and wonder of God is healing. Praise Him with your voice and praise Him with your heart and mind. Borrow or purchase recordings of worship songs to lift you out of the depths of despair into the loving presence of Jesus. Sing softly to the Lord "Great Is Thy Faithfulness" and "Jesus Loves Me."

God extends His grace and mercy to forgive surly, stupid mistakes. You can give up on yourself only if He does, yet He will never give up on you. Forgive yourself because He has forgiven you. Invite back and serve those you have hurt, and watch God perform relational, emotional, and spiritual healing. Most of all, in the middle of your horrific loss, make the worship of Christ the centerpiece of your life. Worship fuels faith, heals hearts, and calms fears.

He is waiting to receive your worship and praise—a sweet fragrance to Him, holy and acceptable. Your praise to God will become a pillow of rest to your head, and your focus on the Lord's majesty through worship will remind you of your utter dependence on Him. Worship God in the middle of your pain and worry, and then receive by faith the wonders of His grace!

Come, let us bow down in worship, let us kneel before the LORD our Maker (Psalm 95:6).

Am I engaged in regular personal and corporate worship of my Lord Jesus?

The Lord Gives and Takes

Naked I came from my mother's womb,
and naked I will depart.
The LORD gave and the LORD has taken away;
may the name of the LORD be praised.

Job 1:21

The Lord gives, and the Lord takes. He gives life, and He takes life. He gives relationships, and He takes relationships. He gives blessings, and He takes blessings. He gives prosperity, and He takes prosperity. He gives opportunities, and He takes opportunities. He gives health, and He takes health.

It is easy to praise God when He gives us good things, but it is hard to praise Him when He takes away good things. When He takes, He still deserves praise. It is the power of praise to the Lord that empowers our faith to endure. Praise to Jesus prompts us to persevere in belief and obedience. He realigns our hearts and minds to heaven's expectations so we will not bow to earth's demands. When God gives, it's a blessing, and when He takes, it's a blessing. He knows our needs.

We count as blessed those who have persevered. You have heard of Job's perseverance and have seen what the Lord finally brought about. The Lord is full of compassion and mercy (James 5:11).

The Lord is full of compassion and mercy. His character is not cruel, but caring. He is not harsh, but kind. The Lord is gracious, not mean-spirited. However, He is jealous for you. He delights in you for who you are, and who you can become by His grace. His loyal love will not allow you to be enamored with someone or something that competes with Him. Christ removes any competitors for your exclusive devotion.

You can be content and grateful for the lot in life God has given you. Perhaps He has you in your current career for the growth of your character and competence. Sometimes He rains down grace, and other times the sun of adversity beats down and causes a sweat of suffering. The Lord gives and takes in His timing and for His glory. Hold loosely His blessings and burdens, and be ready to receive His great grace and love.

Now listen, you who say, "Today or tomorrow we will go to this or that city, spend a year there, carry on business and make money." Why, you do not even know what will happen tomorrow. What is your life? You are a mist that appears for a little while and then vanishes. Instead, you ought to say, "If it is the Lord's will, we will live and do this or that"
(James 4:13-15).

Salvation from Suffering

When Job's three friends...saw him from a distance, they could hardly recognize him; they began to weep aloud, and they tore their robes and sprinkled dust on their heads.

Job 2:11-12

Jesus came to defeat the Enemy by suffering on the cross, not by inflicting violence on the violent. Man's violent act toward Christ turned into God's extravagant love and forgiveness in Jesus. Too often I see photographs of innocent American citizens (and other global victims) whose bloody bodies are riddled by bullets or bomb fragments from cowardly terrorists. My heart hurts. My sense of justice is outraged. Where is God in these ungodly acts?

Yet the Lord's mercy can convert violence into faith in Him.

Job's suffering did not go unnoticed by his friends. Their interaction with him was a wild ride of comfort, condemnation, and conversion. His Gentile friends began by being sympathetic, only to gradually berate Job with accusations of sin based on their perception of his punishment being for pride. In the end, these three arrogant accusers were brought to salvation by the suffering of one (Job 42:7-9). Similar to our Savior, Jesus, on the cross (Luke 23:34), Job remained steadfast for the sake of those who did not know what they were doing. Ultimate salvation from suffering is God's gift to all who trust.

> *It only makes sense that God, by whom and for whom everything exists, would choose to bring many of us to His side by using suffering to perfect Jesus, the founder of our faith, the pioneer of our salvation (Hebrews 2:10 THE VOICE).*

Does your suffering or someone else's seem unfair or unnecessary? If so, by faith seek to see the bigger story of Christ's salvation at work in other needy souls. Our Lord Jesus does not waste pain; the Holy Spirit uses injustice to justify those separated from God in their sin. Your long-suffering is the Spirit's opportunity to draw lost souls to Jesus.

What does the Lord expect of us in the middle of suffering—our own or another's? Our heavenly Father's desire is for His children to draw deeper into Christ's living water from His well of grace. Satan may try to ambush our trust in Jesus with trials and tribulations—or even worse, with fame and fortune—but though our bodies and souls may suffer, we gladly suffer for the sake of the gospel. Suffering is the canvas on which Christ etches His eternal invitation to be with Him.

> *I want to know Christ—yes, to know the power of his resurrection and participation in his sufferings (Philippians 3:10).*

Who needs my comfort and prayers in the middle of current pain and suffering?

A Friend's Misapplication of Truth

Blessed is the one whom God corrects;
so do not despise the discipline of the Almighty.
For he wounds, but he also binds up;
he injures, but his hands also heal.

Job 5:17-18

A good thing misapplied can become a bad thing. For instance, if a medical doctor diagnoses a person with cancer—when in reality, the tumor is benign—then chemotherapy would be unnecessary, perhaps harmful. In the same way, the misapplication of truth can create confusion and hurt, especially when spoken out of judgment and pride. Good words become bad words when they are the wrong words, spoken in the wrong way.

Eliphaz, Job's friend, assumes the worst of his friend and wrongly determines that Job is being disciplined by God for sin in his life. He attacks Job's integrity with a judgmental misapplication of truth. Yes, God's correction is a blessing to His children, not to be despised, but in this situation Job is not suffering because of the Lord's punishment. Instead,

God loves and respects Job's integrity, so He honors him by allowing him to suffer for the sake of righteousness.

> *What you heard from me, keep as the*
> *pattern of sound teaching, with faith and*
> *love in Christ Jesus (2 Timothy 1:13).*

Have you been wrongly accused? Has someone used the truth as a club to your wounded heart instead of a healing ointment applied with words? Be patient and forgiving toward the prideful who are impatient and unforgiving. Your integrity is unassailable in the secure hands of your Savior, Jesus. Have you wrongly accused another out of anger? Go quickly to the one you alienated with your inaccurate, perhaps even smug application of truth. Humble yourself before the one you offended, before the Lord must humble you for your insensitive remarks. Seek mercy.

Truth is heaven's medicine for ailing humanity, but it's to be carefully mixed with a healthy portion of prayer and humility. Preachers and teachers, beware of using truth as a bully pulpit or a public exhibition of your intelligence and communication skills. Those who present the Word of God like Paul did do so with fear and trembling. Handle truth with care, mercy, and humility so you might be handled with care, mercy, and humility. First apply truth to your own heart; make it a habit.

The wise willingly apply unchanging truth in a changing world.

Do your best to present yourself to God as
one approved, a worker who does not need
to be ashamed and who correctly handles
the word of truth (2 Timothy 2:15).

What truth is the Spirit seeking to teach me? How
can I appropriately teach others?

Feeling Unheard, Yet Heard by God

Do you mean to correct what I say,
and treat my desperate words as wind?
You would even cast lots for the fatherless
and barter away your friend.

Job 6:26-27

We all want to be heard, for our ideas to be valued. But when we feel unheard, especially by friends, our hearts can slump into an unhealthy posture of dejection. We ache. From time to time we all need correction, but not to the point of contempt, where it seems like every time we open our mouth, our antagonist attacks us. In one season in my work, I felt totally unheard. My supervisor acted deaf, and the intimidation and innuendos were painful to my heart and sickening to my soul. Eventually, we parted ways; sadly, we never fully understood each other.

Job finds himself in a situation where he feels totally on the outside of a relationship that once throbbed with passion and possibilities. He tries to reason with an unreasonable person—Eliphaz—but Job's integrity is being attacked. Like a swirling wind captures a feather, once Job's words cross his lips, they are swept away and dismissed by a mind already made up. He tries to claw back with a straightforward and stingingly accurate civil discourse, but he learns that unfair accusations need to be addressed with a prayerful, direct response. Integrity hears and then speaks!

He who walks in integrity and with moral character walks securely, but he who takes a crooked way will be discovered and punished (Proverbs 10:9 AMP).

Do you feel unheard, misunderstood, or misrepresented? If so, be patient and pray. Don't become like the one who makes you feel undone. Ask the Lord what He wants you to learn. As you experience a crucible of sadness, seek quiet but honest introspection. Ask the Holy Spirit to burn away the unnecessary and leave only what's necessary for Christ's purposes. By faith you learn to scale the mountain of God's will in the valley of death to self. Humility listens and learns.

By God's grace, seek to speak the truth with patient, nondefensive clarity. Courageously practice saying out loud what you feel, what you shouldn't do, what the truth is, and what you should do. For example, say out loud, "I feel disrespected. I want to attack. But in Christ, I am respected."

An unheard heart must express its deep desire for an honest hearing. Rest assured that God always hears you.

> *This is the confidence we have in approaching*
> *God: that if we ask anything according to*
> *his will, he hears us (1 John 5:14).*

Finding Assurance in Adversity

> If I have sinned, what have I done to you,
> O watcher of all humanity?
> Why make me your target?
> Am I a burden to you?
> Why not just forgive my sin
> and take away my guilt?
>
> *Job 7:20-21 NLT*

A person may not feel assured of their salvation, but feelings can be an unpredictable indicator of truth. Objective certainty grasps the facts of the principle itself, while subjective belief is based on what I might think or feel. The assurance of my salvation is total trust in my heavenly Father to forgive and pardon me of my sin based on my faith in Jesus Christ as my Savior.

Job struggles with his assurance of God's forgiveness because his mind and emotions have been whipsawed back and forth into a faithless frenzy. His friends condemn him for his perceived sin, and heaven seems deaf to his prayers as he pours out to the Lord in his unmerited suffering. Job lacks assurance of salvation not because his faith is not genuine, but because he has succumbed to subjective feelings of guilt and fear that flow from his horrendous circumstances. Life can crush us into a state of confusion, while we still desperately cry out to Christ for clarity.

> *I, even I, am he who blots out your*
> *transgressions, for my own sake, and remembers*
> *your sins no more (Isaiah 43:25).*

Christ offers calm assurance in the middle of circumstantial chaos. Out of confusion, you may ask, "Where do I go? What do I do?" Relational conflict may have caused your resolve for decisions of integrity to reach a breaking point of emotional collapse—you feel viciously attacked by outside forces. First take a deep, spiritual breath, and then exhale fear and inhale faith. Do not allow panic to take your mind and heart to a worst-case scenario. Instead, hope in the Holy Spirit to do a work of grace in your heart. Assurance comes to a submitted soul.

Humility of heart is your default when you feel no one understands your situation. A humble spirit is not afraid to admit its mistakes and ask for help, nor does it demand to have its way. You do not have to do what the world says is important to be important. Be faithful where the Lord has you, and be assured you are valued and cherished by your Savior, Jesus. Let your humility grow your heart of patience with other people.

Salvation's assurance ensures the humble.

> *Blessed [spiritually prosperous, happy, to be admired] are the poor in spirit [those devoid of spiritual arrogance, those who regard themselves as insignificant] (Matthew 5:3 AMP).*

How can I grow in humility in my expectations of others?

A Reliable Trust

> What they trust in is fragile;
> what they rely on is a spider's web.
> They lean on the web, but it gives way;
> they cling to it, but it does not hold.
>
> *Job 8:14-15*

Temporal trust is fleeting and deceptive. It looks like a safety net, but when you lean on it, it gives way. For example, you can trust in a good boss for your employment. However, your boss may receive a promotion or leave the company altogether. Don't believe your job security revolves around a person or an institution. Trust in what you can see, and you'll be disappointed. Trust in what you can't see, and you'll be fulfilled.

Trusting in God is like being an instrument-rated pilot who flies through the night. The flickering lights illuminating the ground can be misleading. The accuracy of the pilot's instrument panel is what can be trusted. Otherwise, the pilot may land on a well-lit freeway instead of on the safety of an airstrip. Also to be trusted are the instruments of prayer, God's Word, and wise counsel. Good things happen to those who wait on God, so remain patient.

> *Trust in the LORD with all your heart and*
> *lean not on your own understanding; in all*
> *your ways submit to him, and he will make*
> *your paths straight (Proverbs 3:5-6).*

Refrain from moving forward until you know the exact longitude and latitude of God's will. The last thing you want to do is land prematurely or, even worse, crash and burn. Trust in God. He is trustworthy. You cannot see Him, but you can see His evidences all around you—the marriage He healed, the body He made whole, the job He provided, the soul He saved, and His answers to prayer. These evidences shout of God's workings all around you.

You can count on the fact that Christ is at work all around you and in you. He has not left you alone. Trust Him with your parent with whom you currently have no relationship. Trust Him with your prodigal child or with friends who can't seem to find their way. Give your loved ones space; let them learn for themselves what it means to lean on their heavenly Father.

Trust in the unseen rather than the seen, and then the seen becomes all the more beautiful and useful for God's purposes.

> *We fix our eyes not on what is seen, but on what*
> *is unseen, since what is seen is temporary, but*
> *what is unseen is eternal (2 Corinthians 4:18).*

What temporal trust limits my trust in the Lord? How is He working around me?

Laughter Is Good for a Hurting Heart

He will yet fill your mouth with laughter
and your lips with shouts of joy.

Job 8:21

Laughter is from the Lord, His medicine for the mind and therapy for the soul. The Lord laughs because He is the dispenser of laughter. You cannot give what you do not have, and He has plenty to laugh about. Just as an engaging parent intently observes his children, so God sees our hilarious antics and behaviors. The Lord must laugh when He sees one of His children smile and do something silly, harmless, and lighthearted. Indeed, He knows laughter is one way to get us through life's intense moments. God is not so serious that He cannot smile and laugh.

How could Jesus have been 100 percent human if He hadn't experienced an old-fashioned belly laugh? Just hanging out with impetuous Peter would be reason enough to giggle under His breath, or even burst into raucous, roaring laughter. Indeed, God has a sense of humor, and you don't have to look beyond the mirror to verify this fact. His joy and laughter are a refreshing combination. In a day when proud piety has frowned on laughter, God still laughs, and so can you.

God has given you permission to laugh. In fact, He has put joy in your heart and laughter on your lips for a purpose. When you laugh, you relax. When you laugh, the cares of this world shrink, and the Lord looms larger. When you laugh, you learn to enjoy life and the Lord Himself.

Throw back your head and begin by laughing at yourself. Take yourself less seriously and God more seriously. A good laugh lends itself to longer and better living. Lean on the Lord and make His joy your strength.

Laughter infuses your faith with mercy and hope. You are not a naive, laughing fool, but a joyful follower of Christ. Take time each day to laugh at yourself and to laugh with others. Recognize laughter as the Lord's way of leveraging a balanced and healthy life. Life without laughter is dull and mundane. Therefore, choose to lift others and yourself with a good laugh. Laugh often—and do it well.

The Lord may be laughing right now, so smile.

A time to weep and a time to laugh, a time to mourn and a time to dance... (Ecclesiastes 3:4).

What area of my life do I need to take less seriously? Where do I need to take the Lord more seriously?

Hope Brings Security

You will be secure, because there is hope;
you will look about you and take your rest in safety.

Job 11:18

Feelings of insecurity creep into my thinking when my hope fades. I feel insecure with finances when there seems to be no hope for future provision. I feel insecure with relationships when there seems to be no hope for reconciliation. I feel insecure with problems when there seems to be no hope for solutions. I feel insecure with my hurting heart when there seems to be no hope for healing. Insecurity follows hopelessness. Thus, I am not scared when I am hopeful in my heavenly Father's practical wisdom; instead, I am secure in His loving provision. Hope provides security.

Job was on the verge of hopelessness. Having lost his family and his material wealth, he wondered what could be worse. Then to make matters worse, his friends offered little comfort, only a critique of how he needed to change and make things right with God. Fortunately, Job's faith remained in the Lord. He kept his gaze fixed on God above and only glanced at his tumultuous circumstances below. Security in our Savior keeps us from being scared.

When you lie down, you will not be afraid; when you
lie down, your sleep will be sweet (Proverbs 3:24).

Are you facing an unsettling situation that promotes fear-induced insecurity? Fear can easily imagine the worst-case scenario. You become frantic over what-if outcomes, to the point that your fears become a self-fulfilling prophecy. When your soul is spiraling downward, intentionally spend time with hopeful people. The company of misery will only compound your insecurities. As you would with good medicine, inject hope into your soul, and security will spring to life.

Moreover, a secure soul makes a point to see its imperfections as necessary on the canvas of Christ's creation. What we see in the present is only a partial portrait of what the Spirit is painting for the future. So we rest secure, knowing we are in the safe confines of our Savior's studio of sanctification. Developing into the likeness of Jesus is a messy but profitable process. God is our unchanging hope. He is our dependable rock of security. We rest in Christ—secure, not scared.

We who have fled to take hold of the hope set before us may be greatly encouraged. We have this hope as an anchor for the soul, firm and secure. It enters the inner sanctuary behind the curtain, where our forerunner, Jesus, has entered on our behalf (Hebrews 6:18-20).

Humiliation Changed to Humility

I have become a laughingstock to my friends,
though I called on God and he answered—
a mere laughingstock, though righteous and blameless!

Job 12:4

Humiliation is deeply painful. Humiliation comes when embarrassment is prolonged and prestige and status are lost. It is a confusing state to live in. People relate to humiliation like leprosy. Humility is admired while humiliation is looked upon with suspicion, even disdain. At best it receives pity. It's ominous to just survive in shame.

People you thought would be at your side during this time of disgrace have walked away. Their excuse is they don't know what to say. This may be true, but beyond their speechlessness is a fear of association with failure. They are afraid others will think they are condoning your situation or that others will see them as afflicted with your same ailment. You are mortified. You feel abandoned by God and betrayed by people.

Let God love you through this hard time. As Job lamented, "'Though he slay me, yet will I hope in him'" (Job 13:15).

You are on the precipice of depression, and it's entirely possible you have fallen over its edge. You feel paralyzed—bewildered. But your life may not be as bad as it seems. Do you have your health? Does the Lord love you? Are you still in business? Maybe you have blown it beyond belief, and to your chagrin you find yourself at the lowest point of your life, but what humiliation tears down, humility can build back up in Christ.

God is our God of multiple chances. He understands, forgives, loves, and brings beauty out of pain. You can do nothing to erase the past or clear up all the misunderstandings. What you can do is allow God to use this time of shame to bring Him fame. He can be trusted, and He is faithful even through the depths of despair. Our hope is in Jesus Christ. Every pseudo hope brings disappointment and delayed pain. Turn to your empathizing Jesus, and He will soothe and heal your soul.

We have an obligation to give hope to those hung up in humiliation. Do not try to diagnose their situation. Rather, pray for them. Be there to listen to them while also pointing them back to Jesus. Help transform their humiliation to humility by restoring them.

> *Brothers and sisters, if someone is caught in a sin, you who live by the Spirit should restore that person gently. But watch yourselves, or you also may be tempted (Galatians 6:1).*

Have I allowed the Lord to transform my humiliation into humility? What humiliated person can I humbly serve?

Embrace and Celebrate Life

A person's days are determined;
you have decreed the number of his months
and have set limits he cannot exceed.

Job 14:5

The older I get, the more I'm grateful to God for another year on earth as His ambassador. My last day here may be tomorrow or 20 years from now—only the Lord knows. In the meantime, I want to make a big deal about another birthday because it is truly a gift from my heavenly Father. Our family celebrates birthdays with a nice dinner.

After the meal, we take time to honor the one being celebrated by describing their character traits we admire. At the conclusion of our time, they tell us about their "spiritual birthday" experience.

Job reflected on the limitations of his days. His Creator calculated the number of breaths he would breathe. His earthly parent might forsake him, but not his heavenly Father. The One who sets the finish line of life also celebrates our lives while we are here. A healthy diet and consistent cardio workouts can get us only so far—ultimately, we cannot exceed our allotted time on earth. Job knew that only God knew how long he had to live. Yet he chose to worship his Creator and trust Him with his life.

Though He slay me, yet will I trust Him (Job 13:15 NKJV).

It takes time and thought to prepare a meaningful birthday celebration for those you love. For small children it can be as simple as waking up to a room full of balloons, potting a plant together in their honor, or giving them yeses for three things they want to do. For adults it could be hiding multiple birthday cards around the house to be discovered throughout the day and an afternoon massage, capped off with a nice dinner. But a birthday celebration also thanks God for His unique gift!

Birthdays are a reminder of how much our heavenly Father loves us. He brought us into the world, having known us before our conception. Remarkably, in our mothers' wombs He continued our intimate relationship, and birthdays remind us of our beginnings with God. The Lord set us apart for His purposes, and we are the most fulfilled when we fulfill the original intent of our being: to enjoy our Maker and make much of Him. We were born to live for the Lord, to die with the Lord, and to go be with the Lord. Birthday celebrations celebrate our life in Christ.

Before I formed you in the womb I knew you, before
you were born I set you apart (Jeremiah 1:5).

Benefits of Brokenness

My spirit is broken,
my days are cut short,
the grave awaits me.

Job 17:1

Brokenness is a prerequisite to God's thorough usefulness. Before brokenness, we were still self-sufficient and self-dependent without authentic humility. Humility was either false or nonexistent. Before brokenness, anger lurked in the corner of every situation that did not go our way. Then it pounced on unsuspecting victims.

Before brokenness, prayer was a routine rather than a necessity. Our fellowship was not sweet and refreshing.

Before brokenness, our life could be explained by our own efforts, with no resurrection power harvesting results. Rather, results were rooted in our limited strength. Before brokenness, a subtle spiritual pride intimidated or impressed others by our "wisdom," instead of us pointing them to the author of wisdom.

> *The LORD is close to the brokenhearted*
> *and saves those who are crushed in spirit*
> *(Psalm 34:18).*

Brokenness is the rite of passage to blessings, a bridge to the depths of God's love and intimacy. Yet brokenness is not without discomfort, even pain. Brokenness seems like failure on the surface, but on the contrary, it positions us for success. The will of a sleek, stubborn, and strong-willed stallion must be broken before it can benefit its riders. Our full potential can't be unleashed without heaven's taming. Let God break your will before it breaks you. His desire is not to chronically crush your spirit, but to break your will. His goal is to tame your stubbornness.

We miss the Lord's best without brokenness. In some ways, life is a process of "three steps forward and two steps backward." We make progress, but not without messing up. We will repeat some mistakes, and sometimes it takes a protracted time for us to "get it." However, some of us need brokenness to come on us with God's loving intensity. Without Him arresting our attention, we tend to move through our

Christian life nonchalantly. Our bad habits never change, and we settle for behavioral modification instead of Christ living through us with His resurrection power.

Without the fruit of the Holy Spirit, there is no brokenness. Pray for God to break your will; He will not break your spirit. Your spirit is where hope resides. Your spirit communes with God. Your tamed spirit trusts in Him. Let go and let God break you and make you into the image of His Son, Jesus Christ. What He breaks, He makes, and what God makes is beautiful!

> *He heals the brokenhearted and binds*
> *up their wounds (Psalm 147:3).*

Have I experienced true brokenness? Have I allowed the Lord to heal my heart?

What to Do When You Can't Find God

I go forward, but He is not there,
and backward, but I cannot perceive Him;
when He works on the left hand, I cannot behold Him;
when He turns to the right hand, I cannot see Him.

Job 23:8-9 NKJV

In Job 23 we find some of the most honest and transparent words in the Bible. Rather than a song of praise celebrating the nearness of God, this is the lament of a broken man who is struggling to find God amid his pain. Job simply cannot pretend all is well. He can't find the strength to put on a happy face. He cries out from a place of desperation, sorrow, and fear. Yet in the two verses below, Job teaches us two profound truths about following God.

> *He knows the way that I take; when*
> *He has tested me, I shall come forth*
> *as gold (Job 23:10 NKJV).*

Even when Job can't sense God's nearness, he rests in the confidence that he is never abandoned or forgotten. Though we may struggle at times to sense God's direction and presence, He never struggles to find us or care for us. In Him we "live and move and have our being" (Acts 17:28).

> *My foot has held fast to His steps; I have kept His*
> *way and not turned aside (Job 23:11 NKJV).*

The Christian life is often called a journey of faith. At times this journey brings great joy and delight, yet at times we are crippled with grief, sorrow, or doubt. Job reminds us that in these moments, even when life is hard and painful, we must continue on the journey!

Our emotions can be tricky and misleading. They want to tell us what we feel is right, but that might not be true!

When you are struggling in your faith, tell yourself what you know to be true, even if you don't feel it. Remind yourself that God is with you (Isaiah 41:10), that He will never leave nor forsake you (Deuteronomy 31:6), and that He loves you, even to the point of dying for you (Romans 5:8). Navigate seasons of doubt and uncertainty through faithfully living by what you know to be true, even if your emotions struggle to keep up.

Commit yourself to a life of prayer and Scripture reading. Fellowship with other Christians, and let the presence of Christ in them renew and refresh you. Focus less on your own needs, and instead love others just as you have been loved in Christ.

> How can the book of Job encourage me when I struggle on my journey of faith?

Our Dark Side During Dark Days

The eye of the adulterer watches for dusk;
    he thinks, "No eye will see me,"
    and he keeps his face concealed.
In the dark, thieves break into houses,
    but by day they shut themselves in;
    they want nothing to do with the light.

Job 24:15-16

Everyone has a dark side that flirts with feelings and tries to lead them astray. It is ironic that your dark side engenders fear and, at the same time, a false and hollow hope. This dark side is always attempting to seduce you into your old way of thinking and doing. It wants to pull a dark cloud over your soul and rain down discontent and confusion.

The dark side is filled with demons of discouragement seeking to seduce you into poor and even foolish decision-making. It knows that one devastating decision can mark you for a lifetime. The dark side offers the illusion that adultery is harmless and recreational. It reasons with you that, in the cloak of darkness, no one will ever find out. You are led to believe that enough lies can cover up your dark deeds.

> *You may be sure that your sin will find*
> *you out (Numbers 32:23).*

Your dark side will hound you until you get to heaven, so in the meantime, it is imperative to live in the light of God's love. That's where you are accepted and kept secure. Live in the light of accountability, for that's where you have boundaries from the edge of darkness. Live in the light of Christian community, for that's where others can pray for you and with you. Live in the light of God's Word, for that's where you gain His wisdom and perspective.

You can gain authentic energy and excitement only in the light. This far exceeds the artificial tantalizing that comes from submission to the dark side's temptations. No sin can be hidden from God, no matter how concealed it may seem in the deepest corner of darkness. Wise ones submit to the light rather than to the deceptive dark side. The dark side is full of unpleasant surprises, while the route of the Holy Spirit offers pleasant ones. Walk in the light together, as overcomers with God and people. Alone, you backslide into your dark side, so surround yourself with lovers of the light. In the light you get it right.

If we walk in the light, as he is in the light, we have fellowship with one another, and the blood of Jesus, his Son, purifies us from all sin (1 John 1:7).

What area of my life do I need to expose to the light of God's love?

Seek Valuable Wisdom Over Wasteful Worry

Where can wisdom be found?
Where does understanding dwell?
No mortal comprehends its worth...
And he said to the human race,
"The fear of the Lord—that is wisdom,
and to shun evil is understanding."

Job 28:12-13,28

Wisdom is like investments of money, as its value compounds over time. When we regularly add wisdom to our lives, we become wealthy in the ways of God. What is wisdom? Why is it so valuable? Wisdom is the ability to discern right from wrong and to understand what is true and lasting. It exposes the Devil's deceptions and lies. Wisdom frees us to know God's ways.

A life built on the foundation of wisdom can withstand the winds of change and the waves of adversity. Wisdom keeps you engaged with God's perspective. It is a life preserver for the drowning, a compass for the lost explorer, and a light in a dark and perplexing situation. A price must be paid in the process of its discovery and acquisition, but once wisdom lodges in minds and hearts, it grows wise, humble leaders.

As followers of the Lord, "we have the mind of Christ" (1 Corinthians 2:16).

Wisdom's value does not fluctuate with the stock market; it consistently increases over time. Gray hair does not guarantee wisdom, but examined experience does position you to obtain wisdom. It is possible to be an old fool or to be wise beyond your years. Young or aged, highly intelligent or possessing an average IQ, you can gain wisdom. Seek out the wisdom of God, and you will find it. This eternal intentionality with holy aggression pays divine dividends.

Wisdom begins and ends with the fear of God. The truly enlightened engage God in the equation of life. Indeed, you fly life solo without your Savior's insights. The fear of God means you involve Him in your attitude and actions—you meditate on His ways and His truth.

By God's grace, wisdom allows you to synthesize multiple options into the best course of action. Wisdom can take a complex situation and offer simple solutions. It has the uncanny ability to cut through the layers of agendas and motives to the real issue. Wisdom is a no-nonsense defender of common sense and truth. It is practical. However, wisdom resides with God, so seek out wise individuals who humbly depend on God, who give Him the credit for the wisdom entrusted to them. Humility mixed with wisdom overcomes wasteful worry.

To God belong wisdom and power; counsel
and understanding are his (Job 12:13).

Am I intentional to seek out the wisdom of God in my daily life and work?

Compelled by the Spirit Through Suffering

I am full of words,
and the spirit within me compels me.

Job 32:18

God wants us to live a life where our spirit is compelled by His Spirit. When the Spirit within us says yes, we are obliged to follow His lead. It may interfere with our comfort, it may cause us to say no to other good opportunities, and it may require us to sacrifice. But because Christ compels us, we come alive to live for Him and to unselfishly serve others.

If to serve is to speak, then speak with grace and boldness. If to serve is to teach, then teach with accuracy and relevance. If to serve is to make deals, then make deals with those you trust and within your area of expertise. If to serve is to share the gospel, then share the gospel with love and acceptance. If to serve is to mentor others, then mentor others with humility and wisdom. If to serve is to invest in your family, then invest in your family with energy and abandon.

Time is short, so do not waste it on projects and people that are not compelling to you. These may compel others, but not you. Go after what motivates you to excellence. You are compelled by the Spirit of God inside you to influence the world outside you.

[The Jews] began to argue with Stephen. But they could not stand up against the wisdom the Spirit gave him as he spoke (Acts 6:9-10).

A compelling life compels others. Your compelling life lifts others out of their apathy and hesitation. You are a force field of hope and courage, and your life becomes more compelling the deeper you go with God. Your character overflows with the fruit of the Spirit, so people can taste the fruit of the Spirit through your life, and it tastes delicious.

So what does it look like to be compelled by the Holy Spirit? Certainly, you are comfortable with God's purpose for your life. Maybe you broker people for kingdom purposes. You may be a stay-at-home parent, a lawyer, a salesperson, a software developer, a banker, a physician's assistant, a teacher, or a politician. Your vocation is not your ministry, but your ministry is your vocation. Whatever God has called you to do, do it in a compelling fashion or don't do it at all. A Spirit-compelled life compels others to follow Jesus.

Barnabas is a biblical example of a Spirit-led person of God. "He was a good man, full of the Holy Spirit and faith, and a great number of people were brought to the Lord" (Acts 11:24).

> Where is the Spirit leading me to serve the Lord?
> Does my life compel others to Christ?

Constructive Conversation Is Two-Way Communication

I must speak and find relief;
I must open my lips and reply.

Job 32:20

Two-way communication is crucial for the health of organizations and relationships. If I don't talk through expectations, then I set up all parties for frustration. For example, I may expect a project to be completed by a certain date, but if I don't monitor the progress along the way, the deadline may come and go with the task unaccomplished. If, however, a system is in place for ongoing feedback, then everyone is clear on where we are and where we need to go. Two-way communication brings clarity.

What about our most important relationships? Do we take the time to interact for authentic understanding of each other's needs? If we are not careful, we can take for granted the very ones we care for the most, and then, in a moment of misunderstanding, become angry in our disappointment. Two-way communication takes time.

Communication that goes both ways requires knowledge and comprehension. If you speak out of emotion before you gain insight into the situation, then you only prolong a productive exchange. Two-way communication is a product of two people listening, understanding, and taking responsibility for their next steps.

Suffering in adversity, Job struggled with this. "Job speaks without knowledge; his words lack insight" one man said about him (Job 34:35).

Two-way communication is also important at home. Perhaps you could incorporate a daily walk with your spouse just to catch up and hear each other's hearts.

Quality communication flows from quantity time to hear and to be heard. Slow down and make sure you not only listen but speak up.

Most importantly, communication with Christ is your greatest opportunity to gain insight and understanding into His heart. If you are too busy to pray, you are too busy. The Bible is His love letter to you. As you read Scripture, do you fill in your name as you read its admonishments? Two-way communication with Him means you desire to learn.

Listen, my son, and be wise, and set your heart on the right path (Proverbs 23:19).

Do I honor others with constructive conversation?
Do I listen intently to the Lord?

Test Words for Truth

*The ear tests words as the tongue tastes food.
Let us discern for ourselves what is right;
let us learn together what is good.*

Job 34:3-4

Words should be filtered, and your first filters are your ears. Otherwise, words can clutter and confuse your mind. Mixed messages to the mind are especially confusing and disconcerting. This is why words must be tested, just as food must be tasted. Some words are bad for your mental health, while others invigorate and energize your thinking. Your ears are meant to be a checkpoint for truth.

Train your ears to value the eternal over the temporal. Educate them to reject lies and invite truth. If you have been told that you are no good or washed up, a bearer of bad counsel has assaulted you. In Christ you are good; in Him there is always hope and potential. Discern the danger of those words and avoid them. Do not allow them into your thinking, lest you become mentally estranged from the eternal.

The time will come when people will not put up with sound doctrine. Instead, to suit their own desires, they will gather around them a great number of teachers to say what their itching ears want to hear (2 Timothy 4:3).

God's words are an effective filter for the words of others. Someone may tell you to trade your reputation for a short-term gain, but you have already heard God and wise people warn you to flee from this promise of fame. The words of the wise should be received promptly and embraced wholeheartedly.

However, the words of fools need not make it past your earlobes. If their foolish pronouncements slip into one ear, send them out the other just as quickly. Vile and wicked words are normally packaged by hurt and delivered with anger, so dismiss them. Post the two sentinels of good sense and discernment at the entrance of your ears. Receive into your mind the best and the brightest in wise thinking and reject the rest. Listen only to words that pass the Holy Spirit's clarifying discernment. Discerning ears automatically drop-kick diseased words away from entering the playing field of the mind.

God also made special ears—the ears of your heart—for testing before you digest His Word, Let God speak to you through prayer and reflection.

> *"Still other seed fell on good soil. It came up and yielded a crop, a hundred times more than was sown." When [Jesus] said this, he called out, "Whoever has ears to hear, let them hear" (Luke 8:8).*

Reassuring Words During Restless Times

Be assured that my words are not false;
one who has perfect knowledge is with you.

Job 36:4

God made His children to need from others reassuring words like these: "I love you"—"I am here for you"—"I am committed to you no matter what"—"I am extremely

grateful for you"—"You are beautiful"—"I admire you"—
"Your work is outstanding"—"You are a special friend"—
"We will not go into debt"—"We will thoroughly pray
before any major decision"—"God is with you."

Reassuring words ratchet up the value of a relationship
because it is not enough to just think or feel committed.
Verbalized care creates confidence and security. Ambiguity
feeds insecure illusions and false fantasies. Pride thinks it can
keep quiet and somehow communicate care, while humility
can't help but speak words of comfort and affection.

> *If anyone speaks, they should do so as one who speaks
> the very words of God. If anyone serves, they should do
> so with the strength God provides, so that in all things
> God may be praised through Jesus Christ (1 Peter 4:11).*

See your speech as a mouthpiece for God. He calls His
children to be conduits of good conversation on behalf of
Christ. What the Lord thinks about your spouse or work
associate is the starting point for discussions. It's not always
about your agenda; instead, reassure people concerning their
goals and aspirations. Reassurance brings emotional rest.

Behavior motivated by fear generally lacks assurance,
so the fearful need to know they are heard and not alone
in their concerns. They feel loved because they hear genuine words from a friend who communicates understanding.
Conversing with care must precede the pronouncement of
truth—indeed, this leads to constructive conversation.

*One who loves a pure heart and who speaks with grace
will have the king for a friend (Proverbs 22:11).*

Most of all, hear the reassuring words of your heavenly Father. He loves and adores you, and He values you as the pinnacle of His creation. You are forgiven and precious to Christ; He is your biggest cheerleader. He says He will never leave you nor forsake you. You are His friend, His servant, His child, and a trophy of His grace. Listen to the Lord's loving words to you, and by faith, you will receive His righteous reassurance.

*Faith is confidence in what we hope for and assurance
about what we do not see (Hebrews 11:1).*

> What words of assurance can I speak to my spouse,
> friends, and those I serve at work?

Evidence for God Energizes Faith

Have you comprehended the vast expanses of the earth?
Tell me, if you know all this.

Job 38:18

What we don't know about creation is as much evidence for God as what we do know about creation. Our knowledge limitations point to the probability of God within the information we have not yet comprehended. How can we dismiss the existence of God when all is not yet known? And if the proof of God cannot be dismissed, why dismiss Him?

If the nonexistence of God is inconclusive, why declare Him not here? We do not dismiss other areas of life as nonexistent or irrelevant if we cannot fully comprehend them. We enjoy the fruits of electricity although we are severely limited in understanding its origin and makeup. But we enjoy the light, heat, comfort, and security it generates.

Every time the sun rises in the east and sets in the west is evidence for the unchangeability of God. Every time we experience multicolor flowers and the vast array of insects, both large and minuscule, is evidence for the creativity of our Creator. Every time a prayer is answered is evidence for God. Every time a wayward life is rescued and put on the narrow path of Christ's righteousness is evidence for the complete powerfulness of God. Every time the human body is explored, discovering all its intricacies, is evidence of God's sophistication and attention to detail. The mountains point heavenward to His majesty, and the ocean waves clap for His glory and praise.

Let the sea resound, and everything in it, the world, and all who live in it. Let the rivers clap their hands, let the mountains sing together for joy; let them sing before the LORD (Psalm 98:7-9).

One day He will re-create a new creation, much like His original paradise with Adam and Eve. He is a creative, masterful artist and brilliant beyond the imagination of humans. We are a dot on His canvas of creation, although an important dot. God does not create anything insignificant, so you can be assured that you are important to your Creator. You are the pinnacle of His creation, and you matter to Him. Enjoy Him in what you comprehend about His creation and trust Him with what is incomprehensible.

Then I saw "a new heaven and a new earth," for the first heaven and the first earth had passed away, and there was no longer any sea...God's dwelling place is now among the people, and he will dwell with them (Revelation 21:1-3).

What evidence around me points to the existence of God? Do I really believe? Do I know how important I am to Him?

Selfless Prayers for Those Snared by Sin

The Lord accepted Job's prayer. After Job had prayed for his friends, the Lord restored his fortunes and gave him twice as much as he had before.

Job 42:9-10

Friends snared by sin need our prayers, not our prognosis. God's part is conviction and life change, while our part is prayer. That is not to say there isn't a time and place to confront a believer living in disobedience. However, we are not the judge—God is. But other-centered praying is freeing for both the person praying and for the person being prayed for. As we pray for others, we are freed from preoccupation with our own problems.

The severity of another's needs can dwarf our own. Through the posture of selflessly praying for another, our perspective becomes healthier and our gratitude grows. We learn to count our many blessings and to be content. Of course, it's okay to ask for God's favor, but not at the expense of excluding prayer for others.

> *Isaac prayed to the LORD on behalf of his wife, because she was childless. The LORD answered his prayer, and his wife Rebekah became pregnant (Genesis 25:21).*

An exciting part of praying for others is the change we experience. Praying for other people cultivates an attitude of love and forgiveness in the person praying. Talk with God often about the needs of others, but be aware that you might become an answer to that prayer. Pray for a friend in financial need, and the Lord may lead you to assist. Pray for a relative whose heart is hard, and God may lead you to soften it with kindness. Pray for a child who has lost a parent, and you may become their parent. Pray for the leadership needs at the church, and you may be called by faith to step into that leadership role.

Most importantly, pray for those outside of faith in Christ. You can do this boldly, knowing it is God's will. Pray that God will use you, circumstances, and other believers to draw another to Him. A stubborn heart is no match for prayer, and Satan's deception is no match for prayer. Pray for sinners to be saved and glorify God.

Brothers and sisters, my heart's desire and prayer to God for the Israelites is that they may be saved (Romans 10:1).

How can I regularly pray for family, friends, and foes for their needs to be met in Christ?

The Blessing of Grandparents

After this, Job lived a hundred and forty years; he saw his children and their children to the fourth generation.

Job 42:16

God gives grandparents the opportunity to be available for their grandchildren. This can be the most fulfilling season of life because of the joy that comes from seeing the third generation follow the Lord with wholehearted commitment. Grandchildren need their grandparents for fun, support, encouragement, wisdom, security, and a loving legacy.

Do you have a plan to be intentional in your grandchildren's lives? Grandparents who take the time to be with their grandchildren invest in the next godly generation. Do you want to be remembered for being available to those who desire you the most or for being busy doing good things for people who probably won't attend your funeral? Bless your grandchildren with your faithfulness to them and the Lord—pray for His will in their lives.

When Israel saw the sons of Joseph, he asked, "Who are these?" "They are the sons God has given me here," Joseph said to his father. Then Israel said, "Bring them to me so I may bless them" (Genesis 48:8-9).

Grandchildren need their grandparents' blessing.

What are grandparents to do if they are available, but the grandchildren are not? Whatever the relational chasm, perhaps a geographical challenge or a generational gap, pray for them to love Christ. Don't allow distance to dissolve your relationship with your grandchildren. Look for creative ways to go to them, such as relieving Mom and Dad for a needed time away. Invite them to join you on an educational trip to an interesting historical site.

Moments with Grandmother and Granddaddy create memories not soon forgotten. Fishing, hunting, baking, reading, learning to drive, walking together, and laughing are all healthy interactions that build a sense of belonging for grandchildren. In a transitional society, it's imperative that families find close community. Perhaps you can pray for a local, "adopted" grandparent who can fill in the gap caused by absent grandparents.

If you are a grandchild, reach out to your grandparents. They will not be with you forever, and they cherish every word of communication with you. Visit them often at their home, call them regularly, and write them nice notes thanking them for their love for you and others. The older generation needs the respect and care of those blessed by their wisdom and generosity. Grandparents deserve honor expressed with our time, talent, and treasures.

> *Stand up in the presence of the aged, show*
> *respect for the elderly and revere your God.*
> *I am the LORD (Leviticus 19:32).*

How can I be available for my grandchildren? How can I honor my own grandparents?

People of Prayer

In return for my friendship they accuse me,
but I am a man of prayer.

Psalm 109:4

People of prayer pray. Prayer is their first line of defense and most effective offensive strategy. Prayer is not an afterthought or a last-ditch engagement with the eternal, but the first thing to come to mind. Prayer is not just a demonstration of discipline and determination, but a desperate dependence on God. It is conversing with Christ, not just asking God for goodies and guarantees. People of prayer enter into intimacy with the Almighty.

People of prayer avoid self-inflicted problems because they pray first. Prayer is medicine for the sick and refreshment for the soul. Prayer may be the best gift you can give someone. You may not have silver and gold to give, but you can give prayer (Acts 3:6). People of prayer do not speak of praying with a simple, "I'll pray for you." On the contrary, with a seriousness of purpose and responsibility, they stop what they are doing and lift to heaven the concerns of the one requesting prayer. As you hear them pray, a peace and calm overcome you.

Start by getting on your knees for five minutes each morning. Prayerful posture is important to people of prayer. Their posture is humble and dependent. Humble yourself daily before your heavenly Father. Lie facedown on the floor, if necessary. Then get up and consider making a prayer list.

Do not sell yourself short by feeling unqualified to be a person of prayer. This role is not reserved for the super righteous. It is for adulterers, liars, and murderers like David.

Have mercy on me, O God,
according to your unfailing love;
according to your great compassion
blot out my transgressions (Psalm 51:1).

People of prayer cannot be pigeonholed based on their appearance, behavior, or speech. They come in all shapes and sizes and God-given temperament. They are humorous and humble, loud and quiet, spontaneous and methodical, creative and concrete, eloquent and simple. However, they are not proud or arrogant. People are their pleasure, and heaven is their home; they check in there often. Jesus is their "go-to man."

Worship, thanksgiving, praise, and adoration permeate the prayers of people of prayer. People of prayer pray.

Pray continually (1 Thessalonians 5:17).

Genesis of Wisdom

The fear of the LORD is the beginning of wisdom;
and all who follow his precepts have good understanding.
To him belongs eternal praise.

Psalm 111:10

The fear of the Lord is foundational to attaining Almighty God's wisdom. Out of holy reverence, heaven opens its doors of understanding. The creation will never begin to understand the Creator until a coming together of minds over who is superior and who is the author of salvation. Once you capitulate to Christ, surrender to Him, this positions you to receive His good gifts, chief of which is wisdom. Your heavenly Father rewards prayer with wisdom from above. Fear of the Lord with a humble request finds wisdom from above.

God's wisdom is also found in God's Word. His precepts are meant to protrude from your mind like road signs on a highway. Sometimes you need to exit for fuel and rest, but other times it is wise to change direction and invite others to join you. To know God, to walk upright before Him, is the greatest of all applied sciences. So wisdom is much more than knowledge; otherwise, education alone would be the answer to all human suffering. Wisdom confesses Christ as Wisdom.

> *It is because of [God] that you are in Christ*
> *Jesus, who has become for us wisdom from*
> *God—that is, our righteousness, holiness*
> *and redemption (1 Corinthians 1:30).*

The life of Christ models wisdom personified. The Holy Spirit gives illumination and understanding to Holy Scripture. Your heavenly Father invites you to ask for wisdom so you can live obediently. Attaining wisdom is for aligning your life around the attributes of Almighty God. You learn to apply what the Lord thinks not only to your life, but also for the benefit of others. Attaining wisdom is not all about you becoming a wise person, but about your life glorifying God to others. Wisdom is a bridge to obedience.

Practical godliness is a test of wisdom, so use your wisdom to mediate broken relationships, foresee problems, serve the team, love your family, and point people to Jesus. Wisdom places faith in Christ out front and humbly deflects attention away from self.

Use wisdom to gain understanding, obey God, and lead people into a growing relationship with Christ. To Him alone belongs eternal praise for His gift of wisdom!

The fear of the LORD is the beginning of wisdom; all who follow his precepts have good understanding. To him belongs eternal praise (Psalm 111:10).

How can I grow in my fear of the Lord and grow in God's wisdom?

Secure in Christ

They will have no fear of bad news;
their hearts are steadfast, trusting in the LORD.
Their hearts are secure, they will have no fear;
in the end they will look in triumph on their foes.

Psalm 112:7-8

Secure servants of Jesus have nothing to prove, for they rest in the pronounced peace of the Lord. Their love for God is deep and wide, and their confidence in Christ is unshakable and uncompromising. Security's only fear is to develop distrust in Almighty God; therefore, it maintains a holy heart, a meditative mind, and a courageous countenance.

Fear tries to seduce security into thinking its Savior, Jesus, is undependable and detached, but God's promises ring true in faithfulness and with intimate concern. This world is always pregnant with bad news, so do not make the world your focus or you will be driven by worry, fear, and insecurity. Trust rests securely as it jettisons fear.

The Scripture teaches, "Let the beloved of the LORD rest secure in him, for he shields him all day long, and the one the LORD loves rests between his shoulders" (Deuteronomy 33:12).

Security is found nestled between the strong shoulders of God. Be hopeful in heaven's track record of trust, and do not be overwhelmed by earth's issues, which are insistent on insecurity. Job understood this in a raw way: "'You will be secure, because there is hope; you will look about you and take rest in safety'" (Job 11:18). Insecure people struggle with this unseen safety net from their Savior because they want to see something of substance. But faith sees the secure hand of the heavenly Father.

The secure stand their ground and remain brave in their beliefs, so stay true to the truth, rest in your integrity, and fight the good fight by faith. Let the reality or even threat of bad news embolden your belief in God. The steadfast triumph!

Furthermore, your security has a ripple effect of reassurance on those around you. Your steadfast faith and joyful sacrifice rub off on your family, friends, and work associates. God is using your peaceful perspective to keep others from panicking. If your security were in your belongings or about your image, you would find yourself struggling with insecurity. So stay focused on your Savior, Jesus, who is stable and secure. The enemy of security is fear, so reject it by faith.

Riches do not endure forever, and a crown is not secure for all generations (Proverbs 27:24).

How can I recognize and embrace my security in Jesus and ignore fear's threats?

The Secret of a Mother's Happiness

He settles the childless woman in her home
as a happy mother of children.
Praise the LORD.

Psalm 113:9

What makes a mother of children happy? Is it just the children? If so, there would be a world of happiness because children contribute to a mother's joy. Jesus said, "A woman giving birth to a child has pain because her time has come; but when her baby is born she forgets the anguish because of her joy that a child is born into the world" (John 16:21).

Offspring should not be the only reason for a mom's feelings of fulfillment. In fact, if a mother's happiness is contingent on her children, she will quickly become discontented. A greater source of happiness is based on gratitude to God and His glory. She can rejoice because God invites intimacy with Him.

Pregnancy is a gift from Providence. The Bible says, "Children are a heritage from the LORD, offspring a reward from him" (Psalm 127:3). Therefore, you can be extremely grateful for the gift of God's child. Your son or daughter is a stewardship from your Savior, not a competition for your time and money. Parenthood is an opportunity to serve, build your faith, and become more like Jesus.

Have you written your heavenly Father a thank-you note for the gift of your child? Happiness comes to mothers who experience hilarious appreciation for the Almighty's entrustment of children. Be eternally grateful for the Lord's unspeakable expression of love through the life of your little one. Of course, children will frustrate you and let you down, just as you have let down your own parents and God. Learn to liberally apply love, grace, forgiveness, and discipline in the same way you administer ointment to their cuts and scrapes. Teach them the truth of Scripture, model faith for them, and joyfully watch as they enter into a personal relationship with Jesus.

The apostle John experienced this joy because of people he discipled: "I have no greater joy than to hear that my children are walking in the truth" (3 John 4). Mothers experience happiness when they praise God for the privilege of being a parent. Your role as a mom is your way to bring glory to God. You smile because you know that as you serve your child, you are serving Christ (Mark 9:36-37). Be happy because your heavenly Father has blessed you. He has given you the gift of His Son for your barren soul and the gift of a child for your joyful service.

Trust During Transitions

When Israel came out of Egypt,
Jacob from a people of foreign tongue,
Judah became God's sanctuary,
Israel his dominion.

Psalm 114:1-2

Timely transitions are necessary to teach trust in the Lord. Spiritually, they move a life from being shackled with sin to being freed up by faith in Christ. Following Jesus is a transition from distrust to trust, fear to faith, insecurity to security, selfishness to selflessness, hell to heaven, being lost to being found, isolation to community, getting to giving, and scarcity living to abundant living.

We move from the darkness of deception into the light of God's love. Obedience to Him transitions us from the foreign tongue of faithless living to the Lord's familiar language of faith. So trust the Lord whether a transition feels forced or is a conscious choice. In either case, Christ is in control; do not settle for a comfortable circumstance if God is calling you to what may feel like an uncomfortable opportunity. Grow and go with Jesus during timely transitions.

> *You were taught, with regard to your former way of life, to put off your old self, which is being corrupted by its deceitful desires; to be made new in the attitude of your minds; and to put on the new self, created to be like God in true righteousness and holiness (Ephesians 4:22-24).*

Furthermore, take hold of a timely transition and accept it as a gift from God. It may be a career move full of fear and possibilities. Pray for a mentor as you make your way into a new field of study or work. A wise mentor serves as a reliable voice of reason and reality in an atmosphere of change, like a father mentoring his son:

> *My son, pay attention to my wisdom, turn your ear to my words of insight, that you may maintain discretion and your lips may preserve knowledge (Proverbs 5:1-2).*

Your timely transition may mean the last child has moved out, leaving you in a lonely house. This is an opportune time to shift your service from inward to outward. Perhaps you can make your home a sanctuary for a young person who has lost their way. Hospitality is a warm way to bring heaven to earth, and a structured and encouraging environment exemplifies the love of the Lord.

Use timely transitions as a trend that is your friend. Trust God as He transitions you to His timing!

The LORD was with Joseph so that he prospered, and he lived in the house of his Egyptian master (Genesis 39:2).

> What transition do I face that requires my total trust that Christ is in control?

Precious to the Lord

Precious in the sight of the LORD
is the death of his saints.

Psalm 116:15 KJV

Saints are special because they are precious in the sight of the Lord. More specifically, He sees the death of saints as precious in His sight. Their faithful living leaves a residue of righteousness in the wake of their relationships. Their countenance reflects Christ as they speak His truth and exhibit His grace. Precious memories remain of those who are precious to Jesus because they leave behind a legacy of having loved well.

As they live, saints provide a picture of Jesus, allowing us to look into the life of our Lord by their godly example. Their sensitive spirits rejoice when we rejoice and weep when we weep. They do not cast stones of judgment; rather, they are rocks of reassurance and encouragement. They are on the lookout for ways to serve and draw attention to their Savior, Jesus, not to themselves. The inner beauty of their character is beautiful to behold. Saints finish well, so their deaths are a celebration of their faithfulness to God.

Let it be the hidden person of the heart, with the
incorruptible beauty of a gentle and quiet spirit, which
is very precious in the sight of God (1 Peter 3:4 NKJV).

Have you lost a precious soul near and dear to your heart? Has a member of your family or a lifetime friend who is like a brother or sister gone to be with the Lord? Someone precious has been taken and given their glorified body, while you remain in a temporary tent that mourns a great loss. Grieve well; God has promoted His precious one.

Saints who die are precious because they have believed and seen Jesus as the most Precious One. Now that they are in the presence of Jesus in heaven, be intentional to enter into the presence of Jesus on earth. Although their bodies no longer live, be inspired that their precious spirits live on to prod you to love God and to love people. Use these defining moments of death to step up to another level of faith, love, and hope that the Lord desires.

The death of your precious saint compels you to continue being precious to God throughout your whole life.

Simon Peter, a bondservant and apostle of Jesus Christ,
to those who have obtained like precious faith with us
by the righteousness of our God and Savior Jesus Christ:
Grace and peace be multiplied to you in the knowledge
of God and of Jesus our Lord (2 Peter 1:1-2 NKJV).

> How can I finish well so my life is even more precious to the Lord at my homecoming into heaven?

In Need of Mercy

His merciful kindness is great toward us:
and the truth of the LORD endureth for ever.
Praise ye the LORD.

Psalm 117:2 KJV

The mercy of the Lord reaches out to the vilest sinner. The breadth of His grace has no boundaries; therefore, we are compelled to erupt in gratitude to God. His mercy is all encompassing of the basest evil and grander than the greatest offense. The Lord's mercy fails not; daily, like freshly baked bread, it is warm and appetizing to all who partake.

Mercy is twice blessed. Paraphrasing Shakespeare, mercy blesses he who gives and he who takes. God's mercy is foundational for all our comfort, and His truth is fundamental for all our hope. Our mandate from God is to be merciful to our fellow man because it makes us more like Jesus. In Christ Jesus, God has shown us great, merciful kindness. He made us alive in Christ.

> *Because of his great love for us, God, who is rich*
> *in mercy, made us alive with Christ even when*
> *we were dead in transgressions—it is by grace*
> *you have been saved (Ephesians 2:4-5).*

Furthermore, as a follower of Jesus, you have daily moments to model and minister mercy. To a restaurant server who messed up your order, be merciful. If you get cut off in traffic, be merciful. If you are embarrassed in front of your friends by harsh and unfair criticism, be merciful. If your child fails miserably, be merciful.

Anyone who does not meet your lofty standards or proud preferences doesn't deserve to be crushed under the pressure of your merciless microscope. Mercy is kind. Pride is defensive, impatient, and merciless. Humility is trusting, patient, and merciful. Emulate the Lord's longsuffering, and you will live a much more pleasant and abundant life.

So speak and so act as those who are to be judged
by the law of liberty. For judgment will be merciless
to one who has shown no mercy; mercy triumphs
over judgment (James 2:12-13 NASB).

Enjoy the benefits of mercy: forgiveness, kindness, benevolence, acceptance, healing, peace of mind, and reconciliation. Mercy is your friend who does not seek to make enemies. Be merciful as your heavenly Father is merciful, and you will experience mercy. By God's grace righteous actions can be reciprocated, so be merciful for Christ's sake.

Be merciful, just as your Father is merciful (Luke 6:36).

Where would I be without the mercy of God and others? To whom do I need to extend that same mercy with forgiveness and acceptance?

Pushed Back but Pulled Up

I was pushed back and about to fall,
   but the LORD helped me.
The LORD is my strength and my defense;
   he has become my salvation.

Psalm 118:13-14

Life can be a sequence of pushbacks. People push back, projects push back, progress pushes back, and circumstances push back. Sometimes it seems as though everything and everyone is pushing back. How you respond to those pushbacks will be the difference between living in peace or in turmoil. It is wise to walk in lockstep with the Lord during a pushback period. Let Him be your help and strength. You will drive yourself crazy trying to determine all the reasons around the pushback.

God is still working during this pushback period, so use this time to gather more information and get to know and understand all the people involved. Pushbacks buy you time to develop a better relationship and to craft a more accurate plan. A pushback is not a failure, but a time to regroup and do better. More often than not, a pushback should not be taken personally. You don't know everything going on personally or professionally with all those involved. The people involved have their reasons, noble or ignoble. God will judge a person's motive. This pushback may be for your own protection—what is needed to guarantee God's best for you.

*Through you we push back our enemies; through
your name we trample our foes (Psalm 44:5).*

However, you need to prayerfully push back when necessary. This is part of the maturing process. Say no if your heart is not in this opportunity. Many people have wonderful life experiences to offer you. Some contribute to God's best, and some are just expedient for them. Push back against those people who are too pushy. Help them understand your true feelings and aspirations. Your pushback may be what it takes to persuade others to do the same. Why make changes in the future when you can push back now and start off on the right foot?

Relationships void of pushbacks are fragile and unpredictable. Relationships peppered with pushbacks are resilient and authentic. This is how you get to know each other. This is how justice can bubble to the top, so receive pushbacks as from the Lord. A gentle pushback from the Holy Spirit in the beginning is much better than a shove by the Spirit later down the road. Be prayerful and discern whether God is pushing back or pulling forward. The Lord is your help.

> *[The angel] said, "This is wickedness,"*
> *and he pushed her back into the basket*
> *and pushed its lead cover down on it*
> *(Zechariah 5:8).*

What situation am I facing that requires me to prayerfully and lovingly push back?

The Gift of Today

This is the day the LORD has made;
we will rejoice and be glad in it.

Psalm 118:24 NKJV

Every day is a new gift from God, created by Him and for Him. The dawning of each day displays the light and love of the Lord's creation. Christians celebrate Sunday, the first day of the week, as a reminder of the Almighty's achievements, namely the resurrection of Christ. However, the workweek does not need to be focused on worldly agendas alone.

Seize today as a trust from Almighty God and steward it with a sense of divine destiny. Perhaps you can pray over a blank sheet of paper or computer screen, and then list by faith how you believe the Lord wants you to focus your time. Follow through with the difficult assignments first, execute some easy ones, and then trust God and others with the tasks out of your immediate control. Today has enough time for you to accomplish His agenda.

Teach us to number our days, that we may
gain a heart of wisdom (Psalm 90:12).

Receive God's gift of today with generous joy and gratitude. Life does happen, but it is much more difficult to be thankful on some days than on others. Sometimes the seeds of sorrow are sown under the dark clouds of confusion, but don't allow fear of the unknown to steal your joy and imprison your peace. Hope in the Lord means you can anticipate His faithfulness during dark times, so be still and listen for His voice.

Today is an invitation to focus on and rest in the faithfulness of your heavenly Father. Adam's sin nature brought a day of sadness, but Christ's sinless nature brought a day of gladness. Live in the moment for your Master, Jesus. By faith and with grateful anticipation, unwrap His gift of today and behold the beauty of its possibilities. Be glad you have only one today, and by God's grace live it to its fullest.

Focus on the next right thing today, and do not become paralyzed with fear of tomorrow. Today is the only day you have, to live, to learn, and to come alive. Seize the day for your Savior, Jesus, and watch Him do a wonderful work of grace. Progress comes in God's timing and in His way. A day dedicated to Christ has more possibilities than a thousand days unrecognized as a gift from heaven.

Unwrap God's gift of today and worship the Giver.

> *Lord, let your ear be attentive to the prayer*
> *of this your servant and to the prayer of*
> *your servants who delight in revering your*
> *name. Give your servant success today*
> *(Nehemiah 1:11).*

How can I receive God's gift of today with peace, contentment, and joy?

Blessed by Blameless Behavior

Blessed are those whose ways are blameless,
who walk according to the law of the LORD.

Psalm 119:1

Christians aspire to a higher standard of behavior, as written in Holy Scripture, and an eternal expectation is woven into their earthly activities. A decision to live this way is not a cold and dry decision, but an adventurous commitment to Christ's life transforming our lives from the inside out. Blameless does not mean sinless, but it does mean heaven does not blush because of our behavior. Indeed, people see us cling to Christ, our Savior, in our struggles.

This pattern of living is quick to confess sin, and by God's grace produces fruit that remains. Blameless behavior is accountable to clear and conservative boundaries around our blind spots of pride and self-destructive proclivities. This life brings a heightened awareness of the Almighty's attributes of holiness and love, and a relentless resolve to righteousness that leads to reward on earth and in heaven.

*This is the account of Noah and his family. Noah was
a righteous man, blameless among the people of his
time, and he walked faithfully with God (Genesis 6:9).*

Furthermore, the Lord promises to bless behavior that
walks according to His law, and so your obedience qualifies
you for benefits that cannot be bought with money or manufactured by human manipulation. Peace of mind is produced when your conscience is clear and your commitments
are complete. Joy runs deep in your soul when you see Christ
at the core of your child's being and in those you love most.

You are humbled and blessed when you are given public
trust to privately administer the truth, love, and wisdom of
God. Your moral authority is a stewardship worthy of quiet
and prayerful attention. Indeed, these liberal blessings of the
Lord invite humility, gratitude, and generosity. Invest His
blessings in others and experience the proliferation of pure
and passionate living.

Above all, blameless behavior begins and ends with walking according to the law of the Lord.

*I have been blameless before him and have
kept myself from sin (2 Samuel 22:24).*

By God's grace, what standard of behavior do I
aspire to? Which blind spot of mine needs focused
accountability?

Freedom Found in Obedience

I will always obey your law,
for ever and ever.
I will walk about in freedom,
for I have sought out your precepts.

Psalm 119:44-45

Obedience creates freedom while disobedience leads to bondage. Our predisposition to seek understanding and application of God's Word is a liberating path. It's when we get off track and act contrary to the ways of the Lord that we become ensnared, like walking through a thicket of thorns. Obedience to God positions us to experience freedom with God.

Obedience is free from the guilt of going against the Lord. We have a clear conscience, having followed by faith the teachings of Holy Scripture. His precepts are profound but simple. His Word is not only wonderful, but it also works. His law is lofty but loving. His decrees denounce sin but give grace to overcome sin. His statutes are a high standard, but they point to salvation in Jesus, and they provide ongoing salvation from sin. The path of obedience, found in the Word of God, leads to freedom.

Sin shall no longer be your master, because you are not under the law, but under grace (Romans 6:14).

Not unlike an earthly father who gives additional freedom to a compliant child, so our Father in heaven extends privileges to His obedient children. Obedience opens doors that disobedience closes; keeping our choices within the confines of Christ's heart may open additional doors of opportunity. For example, cheerful and generous givers might be entrusted with more because they employ God's economic expectations. Selfless people might be given added responsibilities because they will use their elevated role to serve others. Obedience creates freedom to grow.

Furthermore, we obey the Lord by grace through faith. Obedience is not a rigid and cold compliance, but a joyful privilege motivated by love. How can we not obey the One who gave us His Son? We love God because He first loved us, we show our love by following His commands, and we humble ourselves under His mighty hand. He lifts us up to glorify Him in our actions. Despite our imperfect obedience, we can enjoy the freedoms of our gracious heavenly Father. Freedom in Christ comes from obedience to Christ.

*Whoever looks intently into the perfect law
that gives freedom, and continues in it—
not forgetting what they have heard, but
doing it—they will be blessed in what they do
(James 1:25).*

Distress Call to God

I call on the LORD in my distress,
and he answers me.

Psalm 120:1

Some people die a thousand deaths as distress hijacks their hope. It may be the material distress of overwhelming financial pressures or the physical distress of a body accelerating down a path of pain and disease. Relational distress can be traumatic and dramatic as couples feel confined to a crazy cycle of hurt and cynicism. The rough edge of a cruel tongue can sting and sabotage quiet confidence.

What are the next steps when you or someone you love is drowning in distress? Some people want to discuss their distress and accept help willingly. Others struggle to preserve their independence and behave, at least outwardly, as if nothing is wrong. Distress can define you with a humble dependency on God, or it can drive you into a shell of self-pity that ignores Him and others. Reaching out to God in faith provides the best benefits.

*David was greatly distressed because the
men were talking of stoning him; each
one was bitter in spirit because of his sons*

*and daughters. But David found strength
in the LORD his God (1 Samuel 30:6).*

Learn to lean on the Lord during lean times. Go to God first when you are unfairly treated and abused. Wisdom appeals to the Almighty in prayer for insulters, instead of insulting back in prayer-less reaction. Critical backlash against people undermines your character, while compassionate cries to Christ embolden your soul.

Your heavenly Father is prepared for your passionate petitions. Prayer to Him is rewarding and profitable because He will not hear the lie against you, but He will hear your prayer against the lie. His Holy Spirit assures you that He hears and He cares. He is attentive to every detail of your distress, so rest in His reassurance, and your soul will settle down. Above all else, use distress to enjoy your dependency on God.

*You have been a refuge for the poor,
a refuge for the needy in their distress,
a shelter from the storm
and a shade from the heat (Isaiah 25:4).*

How does distress define me? How do the Lord's answers reassure me?

Harvest of Happiness

When the LORD restored the fortunes of Zion,
we were like those who dreamed.
Our mouths were filled with laughter,
our tongues with songs of joy.
Then it was said among the nations,
"The LORD has done great things for them."

Psalm 126:1-2,5

Happiness is found in our heavenly Father. It comes from seeing the big picture of where He has brought us from and trusting where He is taking us. If happiness was contingent on cash and comfort, the modern world would be one laughing lot. However, without heaven as the end in mind, contemporary conveniences work against authentic happiness.

Possessions without our Savior become seductive and controlling, but joy fills our hearts when we think of the Lord's deliverance of us from our captivity in Christless living and into a life of significance. Happiness is the result of giving, not getting; of serving, not being served; and from leading people into a growing relationship with Jesus Christ.

Your love has given me great joy and encouragement,
because you, brother, have refreshed the hearts
of the Lord's people (Philemon 1:7).

Therefore, go forth into life, sow seeds of gratitude and generosity, and you will reap a harvest of contentment and fulfillment. You will garner gladness as you keep serving God and others as your goal for doing good works. Sow the seeds of acceptance and forgiveness, and you will reap a harvest of acceptance and forgiveness.

Do not be deceived: God cannot be mocked.
A man reaps what he sows. Whoever sows to please
their flesh, from the flesh will reap destruction;
whoever sows to please the Spirit, from the Spirit
will reap eternal life (Galatians 6:7-8).

Most people tend to treat you as you treat them, and you can trust the exhausting exceptions with the Lord. Take a risk and get emotionally involved with the needy; you will be happy you did. Surface living is for the shallow, scared, and unhappy. Get below people's facade and feel their pain, weep, and watch God work through your tears as you pray persistently. A harvest of happiness is waiting as you sow selfless service on behalf of your Savior.

The Scripture teaches, "Sow righteousness for yourselves, reap the fruit of unfailing love, and break up your unplowed ground; for it is time to seek the LORD, until he comes and showers his righteousness on you" (Hosea 10:12).

Whom can I joyfully serve and bring a harvest of happiness to everyone involved?

Built by God

Unless the LORD builds the house,
the builders labor in vain.

Psalm 127:1

The Lord does not build shabby structures, and what He touches becomes a testimony to His greatness. Relationships built on Jesus Christ flourish because He becomes the reference point for love. A life structured by the Savior can withstand the trials, tribulations, and successes of society. And a business—or ministry or home—with the values of Jesus woven throughout creates a cultural fabric of excellence.

Is the Almighty the architect of your business endeavors? If not, you have a vain business model. Without the Lord's blessing you will lose your way, and eventually the will to continue. Sometimes working harder only drives you further from heaven's help. This is especially true during difficult days, so take an extended time to fast and pray for the Lord's leading.

Make sure your efforts are united under God to achieve excellent outcomes. Adversity exposes inefficiencies, like light reveals termite-infested damage to the dark places in a house. It may be the foundation of your finances crumbling under the weight of debt. If so, avoid further debt and ask your creditors to work with you to resolve your obligations. Honesty and humility are cousins of trust during troubled times.

> *Swallow your pride;*
> *go and beg to have your name erased.*
> *Don't put it off; do it now!*
> *Don't rest until you do (Proverbs 6:3-4 NLT).*

Make sure money is not your master, but the servant of your Master Builder, Jesus. Do not let fiscal pressure force you to take shortcuts and compromise quality. Instead, become more excellent, and you will stand out among average enterprises. Spend your strength for your Savior, labor for the Lord, and vanity will vanquish. The Holy Spirit replaces futility with fulfillment, faith, and freshness. So by God's grace, build a business—or ministry or home—that lasts through economic upturns and downturns.

Let go of people who brought you to this point, but who will not take you to the next level. The Lord can handle providing their next assignment and your next new team member. Cut costs, increase margins, and prayerfully improve your product and services. Hard times are preparation to become better for the good times. Therefore, replace vanity with a compelling vision and any confusion with a clear mission. Build on the foundation of faith in God by praying for the Lord's plan to be preeminent.

Jesus said, "The rain came down, the streams rose, and the winds blew and beat against that house; yet it did not fall, because it had its foundation on the rock" (Matthew 7:25).

> How does God want me to adjust my life and work so that He is the Master Builder?

Cut Free

The LORD is righteous;
he has cut me free from the cords of the wicked.

Psalm 129:4

Christ cuts us free from the cords of wicked oppressors. It may seem like the wicked have won at times, but this is the testing of our trust. The obstinate may be an entity of God's discipline to break our pride and smooth the edges of our egos. Then we can see those who oppose righteous ways as an instrument of the Lord to instruct us in how to live by faith.

You may have a family member whose faith is a facade. If so, serve them with authentic and unselfish living. Pray their inauthentic life will lose its appeal, and that they will be cut free from a caricature of Christian living. We have been cut free by Christ, freed to serve Him and others.

For we live by faith, not by sight (2 Corinthians 5:7).

Furthermore, the Lord has cut you free from frivolous and irresponsible living for a life of faith. No longer do you have to roam like an unsure beast, stuck in a purposeless predicament. You have the resources of heaven to help you understand the way. You are cut free from cynicism to find hope, from insecurity to discover security, from greed to pursue generosity, from resentment to extend forgiveness, and from worry to experience peace.

Christ has cut you free from circumstantial faith (based on anything uncertain) to a trust rooted in unchanging truth: Jesus Himself. Do not allow the cords of your circumstances to choke out your belief in God. By faith, invite the sharp scissors of your Savior to slice through your situation, setting you free to live and love the Lord, others, and yourself.

Jesus said, "If the Son sets you free, you will be free indeed" (John 8:36).

Does a secret (or not so secret) sin hold you back from enjoying everything Jesus has to give you? If so, seek His forgiveness and healing. Submerge yourself in the security and accountability of other Christ-followers. You can be unencumbered by earthly weights that hold you down like a helium balloon that can't escape its tether. Go to God and receive His grace that allows you to fly by faith!

*Now that you have been set free from sin and have
become slaves of God, the benefit you reap leads to
holiness, and the result is eternal life (Romans 6:22).*

> From what attitude or actions do I need Christ to cut
> me free?

Clean Slate

LORD, if you kept a record of our sins,
who, O LORD, could ever survive?
But you offer forgiveness,
that we might learn to fear you.

Psalm 130:3-4 NLT

With our Savior, Jesus, we are granted a clean slate when
we bring our sin to the cross. God placed our sin on
His Son for our salvation. Sinfully exposed, we are at the
mercy of Almighty God. His holiness helps us better understand our helplessness outside of heaven, so our King Jesus
extends a full pardon to all who believe, for it is His prerogative to forgive.

Forgiveness is at the forefront of our heavenly Father's
thinking. Our pardon is permanent with God, and He is
ready to forgive in an instant. Go to God with guilt, and

leave lust and lies with Him because He saves and forgives to the uttermost. Invite the grace of God to govern your actions and attitudes. Freed-up people free others to enjoy the fruit of forgiveness.

He saved us, not because of righteous things we had done, but because of his mercy. He saved us through the washing of rebirth and renewal by the Holy Spirit (Titus 3:5).

Having your life's slate wiped clean from sin is even more reason to fear God. It is the fruit of faith as you experience His redeeming love. The fear of God results from gratitude for the grace He gives us. We have a robust respect and awe for the Almighty because He does not rain down judgment. God's grace leads us to such a holy regard for Him that we fear grieving Him with continued sin.

Because you have been forgiven much, forgive much. It is not possible or healthy to keep score with those who have hurt you. So pardon your parents and your pastor, forgive your friends and enemies, and let go of unmet expectations. Your fear of God and gratitude to Him facilitate forgiveness with your fellow man. Christ has given you a clean slate, so you can extend a clean slate to those by whom you feel slighted. Wipe clean the slate of sin with the grace of God that has been given to you, and watch Him, by faith, craft a beautiful picture of forgiveness and love. You can start over with someone because your Savior, Jesus, believes in second chances.

The Bible says, "Bear with each other and forgive one another if any of you has a grievance against someone. Forgive as the Lord forgave you" (Colossians 3:13).

> How can I best express my gratitude to God for His pardon of all my sins?

Hardships Endured

LORD, remember David
and all that he suffered.

Psalm 132:1 NLT

Hardships are meant to point us to heaven, and our hope in heaven is what helps us through turbulent times. Yes, hardship can try our trust in the Lord, but He is our one constant support. The foundation of circumstances may shift under our feet from earthquakes—economic and otherwise—but these temporal tremors need not distract our focus on the eternal.

Christ does not change. His desire is to change us so we become more like Him. His promises and character are consistent and a rock of refuge. In our pain it's okay to plead with God for relief, but we must remember the sufferings of His Son, Jesus, on our behalf. After all, it's on the merit of Christ's afflictions and death that we can approach the Lord for life and love.

> *He was wounded for our transgressions,*
> *he was bruised for our iniquities:*
> *the chastisement of our peace was upon him;*
> *and with his stripes we are healed (Isaiah 53:5 KJV).*

See hardships as heaven's hammer to chip away pride, ego, false beliefs, and unbecoming behavior. We are all a work in progress, in need of the Lord's loving but convicting light to shine on our shortcomings. You can endure hardship because your security is in your Savior.

You will endure any bruising of your reputation because, like Jesus, you are a man or woman of "no reputation": "[He] made himself of no reputation, and took upon him the form of a servant, and was made in the likeness of men" (Philippians 2:7 KJV).

David endured hardships because he was so busy doing the work of the Lord that he did not have time for anxious speculations. Therefore, be consumed with Christ and executing His agenda. You will find little time for worry when all you want is to worship, love, and obey the Lord. Use hardships as an excuse to engage heaven's resources for His glory.

Follow Jesus's example for enduring hardships: "For the joy set before him he endured the cross, scorning its shame, and sat down at the right hand of the throne of God. Consider him who endured such opposition from sinners, so that you will not grow weary and lose heart" (Hebrews 12:2-3).

> How does Christ want to change me during changing times?

Live in Unity

How good and pleasant it is
when God's people live together in unity!...
For there the LORD bestows his blessing,
even life forevermore.

Psalm 133:1,3

It is good and pleasant to live in unity, and bad and unpleasant to live in disunity. Unity is Christ centered, and disunity is people centered. Unity talks with others, and disunity talks about others. Unity is productive, and disunity is destructive. Unity prays to God, and disunity plays with God. Unity is the place where God's blessings are bestowed, and we are positioned to be blessed by the Lord when we are unified around His will.

In unity, envy and agendas are set aside for the greater good of the whole. Fear is marginalized because the focus is on faith in our heavenly Father, not in the methods of men. The Holy Spirit is the mediator of diverse perspectives and opinions, and there is oneness in Christ when He is the object of our unity. Harmony invites heaven's blessing.

He made known to us the mystery of his will according to his good pleasure, which he purposed in Christ, to be put into effect when the times reach their fulfillment—to bring unity to all things in heaven and on earth under Christ (Ephesians 1:9-10).

You may be battling divisive politics in your church, at work, in your family, or at school. Do not be persuaded by personalities or emotion; instead, wait on the truth. Let the facts forge your faith, and do not allow fear to drive you to feud. Accurate information is your ally, so wait on it to back up your beliefs. Let love lead you through the process of unification. Love overcomes petty politics and personality conflicts.

God blesses a motivation of love because He is love. When your relationships are one in heart and spirit, you are ready to be blessed. Trust the Lord to lead you, your family, your friends, and your team members into unity around common principles, values, and behaviors. Unity around Christ causes the world to wake up and watch, wanting what you have. It unleashes the opportunity for the Lord to grow you into an influencer for Him.

Jesus prays for you: "I have given them the glory that you gave me, that they may be one as we are one—I in them and you in me—so that they may be brought to complete unity. Then the world will know that you sent me and have loved them even as you have loved me" (John 17:22-23).

> How can I be a channel of blessing the Lord can use to bring unity out of disunity?

Harmony Is Refreshing

Harmony is as refreshing as the dew from Mount Hermon
that falls on the mountains of Zion.
And there the LORD has pronounced his blessing,
even life everlasting.

Psalm 133:3 NLT

Harmony is heaven's high goal for earthly interactions. Harmony brings out the best in others, and disharmony brings out the worst. Harmony seeks first to know the heart of another, and disharmony only wants its own way. Harmony is motivated by selfless love, and disharmony is driven by selfish ambition. Harmony seeks to serve, and disharmony expects to be served. Harmony has a transparent agenda, and disharmony conceals a hidden agenda. Harmony is humble, and disharmony is proud.

David, as the new king of Israel, probably penned the words in Psalm 133:3 as he sought to unify a divided nation of 12 diverse tribes. The former shepherd reminded his people of the Great Shepherd's blessing that rests on harmonious hearts. Majestically described as refreshing mountain dew, harmony brings life and beauty to all who are drenched in its life-giving liquid. When a soul suffers in a heated valley of discouragement and disharmony, the Lord can rain down His cool refreshment of companionship and care on His beloved. Our Creator brings life and hope out of difficulty.

Harmony is as precious as the anointing oil that was poured over Aaron's head, that ran down his beard and onto the border of his robe (Psalm 133:2 NLT).

Has disharmony hijacked a relationship because someone insists on their way as the only option? If so, take a step back and do not be sucked into an emotional response that only exacerbates the situation. Evaluate what is behind the person's narrow view of multiple options. Perhaps they are reacting out of fear because of a past experience that ended in disaster. Or maybe they simply misunderstand what you are trying to accomplish, and they need you to patiently clarify your purpose and plan. Harmony hears out another, without defensive judgment.

Above all else, are you at harmony with your heavenly Father's heart? Does anything in your heart hinder harmonious, sweet fellowship with Jesus? First confess your sins to Christ and gain unencumbered access to His grace to lubricate your vexing relational interactions. Seeds of discord need extraction. A heart at harmony with heaven is capable of harmony on earth, but a heart unaligned with the Almighty is set up to be out of step with fellow Jesus-followers. Harmony comes when two hearts are unified around the heart of God!

> *How good and pleasant it is*
> *when God's people live together in unity! (Psalm 133:1).*

> Whom do I need to seek out to mend our broken relationship?

Be a Servant of the Lord

Praise the LORD, all you servants of the LORD.

Psalm 134:1

Servants of the Lord have one goal, and that is to serve at the pleasure of their Master, Jesus Christ. It is an honor to represent the vision, mission, and values of heaven. Servants of God are quick to praise Him. They show respect by blessing His name, and they loathe the thought of disrespect in cursing His name. Followers of Jesus think well and speak well of Him. He is the object of their affection, the adoration of their worship.

Servants of the Lord bless the one from whom all blessings flow. They speak well of their Master. Wise servants understand that the purpose of serving God is not just accomplishing work but representing Him in their work. Therefore, toil in trust and do not give up for Christ's sake. You are a servant of the Most High, so hold your head high and maintain a humble heart. He keeps His covenant of love for those who long for Him.

> [Solomon] said: "LORD, the God of Israel, there is no God like you in heaven or on earth—you who keep your covenant of love with your servants who continue wholeheartedly in your way" (2 Chronicles 6:14).

Servants of the Lord also serve those their Master loves and accepts, aligning with the Almighty's interest in people and their needs. He feeds and clothes the poor, so you feed and clothe the poor. He forgives and frees those who sin against Him, so you forgive and free those who sin against you. He seeks and saves the lost with the glory of the gospel, so you seek and save the lost with the glory of the gospel.

Unrecognized service seems insignificant, but it is the most significant service. What others don't see, God does, and He rewards accordingly. The Lord blesses those who bless others on His behalf. Servants of the Lord are significant kingdom builders, so stay put in your service on His behalf. The best service leads others to understand the way to be saved.

May others see you in this same way: "These men are servants of the Most High God, who are telling you the way to be saved" (Acts 16:17).

> How can I serve the Lord with gladness and bless Him and others in the process?

God Knows You

You have searched me, LORD,
and you know me.

Psalm 139:1

God knows everything about us. He knows our dreams, fears, and failures. He knows our noble thoughts and our foolish thoughts. He knows, but He knows with an eye toward eternity. His motive for the use of this exhaustive information is intimacy with His creation. Indeed, His infinite knowledge is an invitation to know Him.

He understands our nature and character way beyond our comprehension. He searches the soul for our sake, not His, for He already knows. We do much better when we sense our Savior is watching, so our first step in accountability is to daily ask the Almighty to search and diagnose our heart. His sensitive searchlight helps us to see our motives and methods from His perspective.

> *May these words of my mouth and*
> *this meditation of my heart be pleasing*
> *in your sight, LORD, my Rock and my*
> *Redeemer (Psalm 19:14).*

God knows you need a job, but He wants you to persevere in the process of prayerful networking. God knows you need a spouse, but He wants you to hold high your standards of conduct and character. God knows you need a house, clothes, or a car, but He wants your faith focus to stay on Jesus and not on possessions. God knows your every desire, so ask Him to embed His wishes into your desires. Through prayer, fasting, and godly counsel, invite the Holy Spirit to align your expectations with an eternal agenda. You trust in the Lord even when you can't completely comprehend His plans. But in time He reveals just what you need to know.

You know God knows, and that's all you have to know.

> *Do not worry, saying, "What shall we eat?" or "What*
> *shall we drink?" or "What shall we wear?"...Seek first*
> *his kingdom and his righteousness, and all these things*
> *will be given to you as well (Matthew 6:31,33).*

You can rest in the assurance that the Lord will meet your needs, although maybe not your wants, and that He knows what's best. Like a parent's love for a child, your heavenly

Father loves you despite your imperfections. When He sees Jesus as your Savior and Lord, He sees the perfection of His Son. He knows this is what you need most, for Christ is all you need.

> *God, who knows the heart, showed that he accepted them by giving the Holy Spirit to them, just as he did to us (Acts 15:8).*

How does it make me feel to know that God knows everything about me, yet loves and accepts me unconditionally?

Avoid Harmful Words When You Are Hurting

They make their tongues as sharp as a serpent's; the poison of vipers is on their lips.

Psalm 140:3

Poisonous words come from a proud heart. In our original state of sin, Satan, the old serpent, infected us with the venom of injurious words. We must watch what we say, or we may regret what we say. People in their anger tend to say what their parents said in their anger—a vicious cycle of cynicism that only Christ can break.

Instead of lashing out with language that stings or is even slanderous, take a cooling-down time for calm and clear thinking. Frustration tends to feed judgmental behavior. When our throats are dry and our blood pressure is up is not the best time to speak, because poisonous words pronounce judgments driven by anger and emotion.

> *A gentle answer turns away wrath,*
> *but a harsh word stirs up anger.*
> *The tongue of the wise adorns knowledge,*
> *but the mouth of the fool gushes folly (Proverbs 15:1-2).*

If you have been bitten by bitter words, apply the balm of first bowing down to Christ. Jesus has just what the wounded soul and hurting heart need. The Holy Spirit helps you discern how you can become better, and He gives you patience, humility, and guidance to know when to wait or when to confront. Victims of poisonous words need the serum of their Savior's love and forgiveness. When applied liberally and regularly, it allows you to handle harsh words with an understanding and nondefensive attitude.

Followers of Jesus are men and women of "no reputation" (Philippians 2:7 kjv). God is who gets the glory and grants a good name. So go to the Lord when your pride has been punctured by poisonous words. Ask Him for faith to forgive and grace to extend pleasant words. Don't allow resentment to fester when you have been wounded by slander; rather, apply the ointment of God's grace.

Moreover, pleasant words work out the hurt and replace it with hope. Words like "I love you," "I believe in you," "How can I help?" and "How can I pray for you?" bring out the best in those who need soul nourishment. Emotions venture back out in vulnerability within a safe environment of encouragement. Offer pleasant words that feed hungry hearts.

> *Gracious words are a honeycomb, sweet to the soul and healing to the bones (Proverbs 16:24).*

What are some pleasant words like "How can I help?" that I can apply to a wounded relationship?

A Righteous Rebuke Grows a Righteous Heart

Let a righteous man strike me—that is a kindness;
let him rebuke me—that is oil on my head.
My head will not refuse it.

Psalm 141:5

A righteous rebuke wins the respect of the teachable and trusting and is seen as an act of love and concern. We all need people in our lives who challenge us with truth. Bold messengers motivated by kindness and correction make us more effective leaders, spouses, parents, friends, and followers of Jesus. The unrighteous smile upon us as they offer cruel flattery, while the righteous do not rest until words of admonition are offered.

We invite instruction from those with integrity because we trust their intentions. Fools resent reproof, but the wise profit from its sometimes-stinging sensation. A righteous rebuke is sweet to the soul; like pleasant perfume, it refreshes and renews. It is a loving act. Immature gossips talk about others; mature friends talk directly to others.

It is better to heed the rebuke of a wise person than to listen to the song of fools (Ecclesiastes 7:5).

Listen to those who want to love you through tumultuous times. It is better to have two people around who tell you the truth than ten who tickle your pride and enlarge your ego. Take the time to listen to godly counsel, and then act accordingly. Gracious men and women do not grow weary of candid friends; rather, they thank God for them.

Your spouse sees things you don't, so pay attention and act. Your children care enough to come with their complaints, so lovingly listen to them. Constructive feedback from friends is wise, so admit where you were wrong. At work, serve your team by listening to and implementing their excellent ideas. Survey your customers, and then adjust toward their needs. Wise leaders see others as the Lord's instruments of instruction.

Do not rebuke mockers or they will hate you;
rebuke the wise and they will love you (Proverbs 9:8).

Above all, Almighty God's loving discipline and righteous rebuke lead to wise living. So gladly repent when you feel a twinge of conviction from the Holy Spirit. Like a child who respects the flames in a fireplace by backing away, so is the wise and humble child of God who steps back from being blistered by sin. A rebuke followed by earnest repentance leads to the sweetest, lasting fellowship with Jesus and trusted friends.

Those whom I love I rebuke and discipline. So
be earnest and repent (Revelation 3:19).

Whom do I need to invite into my life as a candid and trusted adviser?

A Healthy Complaint to Christ

I pour out before him my complaint;
before him I tell my trouble.

Psalm 142:2

A heavy heart needs an outlet to express fear and frustration. If this option is absent, you can experience a loss of perspective and an extended stay in pain. It may be the weight of leadership sapping your joy and testing your trust. The death of a loved one may have sent you into a downward spiral of loneliness. Maybe you feel unappreciated and ignored to the point of painful rejection. Troubles need a trusted and safe outlet.

In these moments of madness, we need a safe place to share our souls. The more we bring our complaints to Christ, the less we will complain to others. We have permission to complain to God. Christ collates our complaints, files them in our folder of faith, and patiently hears our protests like a caring and just judge.

I loathe my very life;
therefore I will give free rein to my complaint
and speak out in the bitterness of my soul (Job 10:1).

Your heavenly Father wants to hear your troubles—not for His enlightenment, but for your engagement with Him. Your trust in the Lord triumphs over troubles as you proceed in the process of prayer. Persevere in prayer, and you will discover your troubles are insignificant in comparison to intimacy with Christ. Don't hold back; your complaint to Christ is your way to relief and recognition of Him. Christ's care and love will move you from chronic complaining to authentic thanksgiving. Offer your complaints as a sacrifice to Him, and He will burn away the dross of fear and anger and replace it with His gift of peace and joy.

Hear me, my God, as I voice my complaint;
protect my life from the threat of the enemy
(Psalm 64:1).

Indeed, look to the Lord as you linger in uncertain days. It is better to vent your frustrations to your heavenly Father than for your soul to stew in bitterness. Complaints to Christ are your opportunity to come clean in your heart and to harness heaven's hope. He listens, He loves, He understands, He consoles, He encourages, and He gives grace. Pour out your heart to Him, and He will fill your heart with His Holy Spirit's comfort.

Jesus experienced this tension: "He went a little farther and fell on His face, and prayed, saying, 'O My Father, if it is possible, let this cup pass from Me; nevertheless, not as I will, but as You will'" (Matthew 26:39 NKJV).

> What complaints do I need to bring before Christ
> and entrust to Him instead of to people?

God Memories

I remember the days of long ago;
I meditate on all your works
and consider what your hands have done.

Psalm 143:5

God memories help us remember what is important in life. The Lord's wonderful works come in a variety of expressions. For example, we may have seen His hand at work during our conversion experience in church or at an old-fashioned revival meeting. Or maybe His answer to prayer arrested our hearts during a contemplative conversation with Him along a quiet creek bed.

Our meditation on the Almighty's activities activates our hearts with faith and hope. When we ruminate on His righteous acts, we tend to feel secure and certain. When our own work leads us to wander, we can still wonder at the works of His hands. He can work through our works despite our failings. A mind always on the move needs God memories to meditate on and be encouraged by.

> *They refused to listen and failed to remember the miracles you performed among them. They became stiff-necked and in their rebellion appointed a leader in order to return to their slavery. But you are a forgiving God, gracious and compassionate, slow to anger and abounding in love. Therefore you did not desert them (Nehemiah 9:17).*

Look through your mind's eye and see in hindsight how heaven has directed your days. His Holy Spirit may have led you to say no to one career opportunity because He had a more significant option in mind. The Lord may have closed one door of higher education and opened another you would not have scripted, but it led to where you met your life mate.

You saw His works in a little baby He may have blessed you with, to nurture and love. Or it may be the memory of being with a grandparent and experiencing God's canopy of creation together. It was here you heard the wisdom of the Lord and felt unconditional love and acceptance.

Use God memories to galvanize your faith and make you more like your Memory Maker, Jesus.

So I will always remind you of these things, even though you know them and are firmly established in the truth you now have. I think it is right to refresh your memory (2 Peter 1:12-13).

What God memories would I do well to reflect on with gratitude and hope?

Four Ways Christ Loves Us (Part 1)

The LORD appeared to us in the past, saying:
"I have loved you with an everlasting love;
I have drawn you with unfailing kindness."

Jeremiah 31:3

The Lord's love is much more substantive than a shallow, sentimental emotion or a feel-good moment—His love reaches into the depths of our sorrows to comfort and to the heights of our happiness to celebrate our joy. The Lord's love cares, corrals, chastens, comforts, challenges, calms, and brings clarity out of confusion. Unconditional, unconventional, and unyielding; rarely early, never late, but always timely is the application of His vast reservoir of everlasting love.

What are some ways the Lord loves His children? We can start with these two biblical images:

Like an Artist Loves His Art

"Can I not do with you, Israel, as this potter does?"
declares the LORD. "Like clay in the hand of the potter,
so are you in my hand, Israel" (Jeremiah 18:6).

Like a Michelangelo block of marble yet to be completely sculpted, we are a masterpiece in the making in our Maker's eyes. Rough around the edges, accented by beautiful glimpses of God's glory, with unrecognizable, unhewn areas, we are a work in progress yet beautiful in our Beloved's eyes. Becoming a sculpture of grace is not without suffering to smooth out sinful habits, relational tensions to grow our trust in God's forgiveness, and answered prayer to expose the highlights of heaven's imprints, all the while bringing clarity to our growing likeness of Christ. He is not finished with us, so by faith we patiently submit to the Potter's hand, which molds us into His magnificent creation.

Like a Shepherd Loves His Sheep

The LORD is my shepherd, I lack nothing.
He makes me lie down in green pastures,
he leads me beside quiet waters,
he refreshes my soul (Psalm 23:1-3).

Ever aware of where his sheep are—close by, watching curiously from the edge of the herd, or aimlessly wandering away and obstinate in their determination to do their own thing—the sensitive shepherd seeks to lead his charges to what's best for them. In the same way, our loving Shepherd looks out for us with His provision of rest, quiet contemplation of His majestic creation, and His life-giving soul refreshment. When we stray, when we wander toward the edge of disobedience, He comes after us with loving discipline.

Give ear and come to me;
listen, that you may live.
I will make an everlasting covenant with you,
my faithful love promised to David
(Isaiah 55:3).

How can I accept and apply God's love for me in the unlovely places of my life?

Four Ways Christ Loves Us (Part 2)

Let the morning bring me word of your unfailing love,
for I have put my trust in you.
Show me the way I should go,
for to you I entrust my life.

Psalm 143:8

The Lord's love initiates and pursues the pinnacle of His creation with an eternal engagement. God's love is all pervasive. In our shame, His love wipes away our remorseful tears. In our successes, His love reminds us of His generous blessings. In our anxious hearts, His love brings a peace that passes all understanding. Nothing can separate us from the love of God. Can sin? No, because the cross of Christ is our bridge back to God. Can death? No, because Jesus rose from the grave to give us life.

What are some ways the Lord loves His children? We continue with two more biblical images:

Like Parents Love Their Child

[The Lord] said, "Surely they are my people,
children who will be true to me";
and so he became their Savior (Isaiah 63:8).

Parental love is expressed in a plethora of ways: discipline, encouragement, teaching, modeling, church involvement, prayer, Bible study, and service. A parent nurtures compassion and harnesses passion, and both are crucial to an emotionally healthy child. Compassion is the motivation to be generous in mercy, grace, and giving, while feeling another's pain with empathy and meeting their needs with helpful resources. Parents care deeply and freely, and they help channel a child's passions into productive outcomes: anger into patient forgiveness, joy into gratitude, physical drive into serving others.

God loves us more.

Like a Husband Loves His Wife and a Wife Loves Her Husband

He has clothed me with the garments of salvation,
He has covered me with the robe of righteousness,
as a bridegroom decks himself with ornaments,
and as a bride adorns herself with
her jewels (Isaiah 61:10 NKJV).

The lasting fruit of marital love is intimacy (emotional, spiritual, physical), joy, peace, and fulfillment. Intimacy is not without heartache, pain, and disappointment, but all the while a man and woman grow into oneness around their unity in Christ. Our bridegroom, Jesus, adorns us, His bride, with the jewels of His character, attracting yearning hearts to our hearts. The garments of our salvation are always in style, causing others to look to the Lord for their hope and peace. Jesus loves us by giving His life to us—for us to love!

May...our God and Father, who has loved
us and given us everlasting consolation and
good hope by grace, comfort your hearts
and establish you in every good word and
work (2 Thessalonians 2:16-17 NKJV).

Who needs me to love them today, while I expect
nothing in return?

Grateful Praise to God Out of Our Pain

Let everything that has breath praise the LORD.
Praise the LORD.

Psalm 150:6

Praise the Lord" is not just an invitation to celebrate gratitude to God and reverently worship our King; it is also a command. Jesus directs us to worship our heavenly Father "in the Spirit and in truth" (John 4:23-24). The pinnacle of praise found in this last of the psalms is an exhortation to praise Him in His sanctuary. We praise him with music, instruments, dancing, spiritual songs, and hymns.

The church's chorus of praise to Christ rises to the courts of heaven. In reverence and thanksgiving, we praise Him for His mighty acts: His creation, for its beauty and majesty; His redemption, for its forgiveness and freedom; and His holiness, for its purity and power. Praise to the Lord reveals the Lord.

Stand every morning to thank and praise the LORD, and likewise at evening (1 Chronicles 23:30 NKJV).

You praise Him for His glory, but in the process, you receive the benefit of His blessings. Praise solicits the blessing of His security and peace. In the act of adoration of His character, you are comforted by His care and compassion. Praise brings peace that flows from a prayerful and sincere heart for God. Praise is the battle cry for believers as they engage the Enemy in everyday life. Praising the Lord is your pronouncement of His sovereign security in your Savior, Jesus. Praise Him while you have breath, and you will bring glory to God.

After consulting the people, Jehoshaphat appointed men to sing to the LORD and to praise him for the splendor of his holiness as they went out at the head of the army, saying: "Give thanks to the LORD, for his love endures forever" (2 Chronicles 20:21).

Grateful praise to God gets your heart in the right mood and your mind confident in Christ. A transaction of trust takes place when you take time to praise and thank the Lord. Make it your holy agenda to worship your Savior and Lord,

Jesus Christ, with a grateful heart, and His work of grace will transform you into His likeness. Grateful praise brings glory to God and genuine joy to His children.

Praise Him, and so will other needy people.

> *The LORD is my strength and my defense;*
> *he has become my salvation.*
> *He is my God, and I will praise him,*
> *my father's God, and I will exalt him (Exodus 15:2).*

What challenge am I encountering that invites me to aggressively praise the Lord?

Unresolved Pain

> He longed to fill his stomach with the pods that the
> pigs were eating, but no one gave him anything.
> When he came to his senses, he said, "How
> many of my father's hired servants have food
> to spare, and here I am starving to death!"
>
> *Luke 15:16-17*

Everyone is a product of pain because we live in a world of pain—no utopia exists this side of heaven. Furthermore, unresolved past pain produces present pain. Conversion to Christ does not automatically wipe away all our pain, but

He does give us the tools—grace and truth—to heal hurts and bring wholeness to our hearts.

What is the source of your pain? Maybe your rebellious child went to the faithless far country to "find myself"—and hopefully in the process will die to self. Selfish children create recurring pain. Your son or daughter left home thinking they had missed out, but you pray that once in the womb of the world, they will miss the security, acceptance, and love at home.

Then I would still have this consolation—
my joy in unrelenting pain—
that I had not denied the words of the Holy One (Job 6:10).

Your pain may be the result of experiencing the pain of another. You may be frustrated because anger spews from a hurting heart, and it's hard to get around their wall of pain. Patient love diffuses pain's explosions. Pain can be ignored for a season, but it will not be denied attention. Husbands and wives can preoccupy themselves with work and children, but when work goes away and the children grow up, how will they relate to each other? Invest in your marriage now, so you can understand, love, and serve your spouse later.

As for me, afflicted and in pain—
may your salvation, God, protect me (Psalm 69:29).

Perhaps you are single and feel slighted from a super dysfunctional upbringing. Your parents did not communicate well, they constantly fought, and your acceptance was based on your performance. You have layers of pain because you are a product of a hurting home. Before marriage, seek out a Christian counselor to unpack your emotional baggage. Invite your heavenly Father to enter into the pain in your heart. Apply the balm of His love and grace; rest in the compassionate embrace of your empathizing Savior, Jesus. The One who suffered in pain on the cross—to heal pain—ultimately resolves your pain.

Surely he took up our pain
and bore our suffering (Isaiah 53:4).

To what pain do I need to administer the grace of God? Whose pain can I enter into with compassionate love and understanding?

Avoidable Pain

The wisdom of the prudent is to give thought to their ways,
but the folly of fools is deception.

Proverbs 14:8

Pain is inevitable in life, but some pain can be avoided with proper preparation. There is no need to add unnecessary pain to relationships with unwise decisions and foolish behavior. For example, it takes much more than a grand wedding to create a great marriage. Promises need to be backed with preparation to carry out commitments.

Wise couples get beyond the emotion of romantic love and become students of each other. They truly accept each other for who they are, believe the best in their intentions, and learn how to best communicate. Premarital preparation is a prescription for a healthy life of marital maturity; however, ignoring past pain compounds present pain. Avoid compounding pain by being healed of past relational hurt.

Confess your sins to each other and pray for each other so that you may be healed (James 5:16).

Avoid the pain of regret. Be wise not to create habits or routines that later cause guilt. For instance, during the parenting season of caring for your children at home, how will you adjust your schedule? Can you maintain a heavy travel schedule and still be available for them? Will some hobbies need to be put on hold until a later date? Be wise not to treat every season of life the same. Keep your commitment to Christ as a constant, yet be willing to flex toward the needs of those around you. People who avoid pain are those who actively pray for guidance from Almighty God. Indeed, pain will always be a part of life on earth; only in heaven are we pain free. Fools rush into pain as kind of misguided martyrs, while the wise learn from pain and avoid its unnecessary injury.

The simple believe anything,
but the prudent give thought to
their steps (Proverbs 14:15).

Some pain is unavoidable—a product of yours or someone else's poor decision-making. Do not wallow in self-pity as a victim of a painful past. By God's grace, confess your sin of holding a grudge and get beyond your anger with forgiveness.

Use pain as a platform to proclaim the grace and love of God. Avoid it through making wise decisions, but when faced with pain, leverage it for the Lord's glory. Wisdom doesn't waste pain.

[Joseph said,] "As for you, you meant evil
against me, but God meant it for good in order
to bring about this present result, to preserve
many people alive" (Genesis 50:20 NASB).

How can I make wise preparations to avoid relational pain? What pain do I have in my heart that needs the Lord's healing?

Productive Pain

Then God said, "Take your son, your only son, whom you love—Isaac—and go to the region of Moriah. Sacrifice him there as a burnt offering on a mountain I will show you."

Genesis 22:2

Pain is synonymous with suffering, anguish, trials, tribulation, adversity, trouble, and hard times. It affects our emotions, minds, bodies, souls, spirits, and wills, for it is indiscriminate in its affliction. Sometimes God asks His children to walk through extremely difficult situations. Indeed, there may be no greater pain in life than to be willing to inflict pain on someone you love; yet this is what God asked Abraham to do with his son, Isaac. This pain presented Abraham with a time to either trust God or trust his instincts for self-preservation. Productive pain finds solutions in obedience to God.

How can pain become your helpful teacher and not your nagging nemesis? First, you begin to learn from pain by maintaining a providential perspective and a teachable attitude. See your suffering as a songbook from your Savior, and learn how to sing these new life lyrics. In the beginning of adversity, you may sound off-key in your complaints. And yes, new can be uncomfortable and embarrassing as you learn to harmonize what heaven has allowed.

We also glory in our sufferings, because we know
that suffering produces perseverance; perseverance,
character; and character, hope. And hope does
not put us to shame, because God's love has been
poured out into our hearts through the Holy Spirit,
who has been given to us (Romans 5:3-5).

Christ is with you in the middle of your loss of a friend, a job, finances, or faith. Seek to learn from the Lord in your suffering, for He does not waste pain. Pain is meant to move you in the direction of your Master. Pain purifies your motives and validates your obedience. Convenient obedience can be shallow and insincere, but pain verifies authentic obedience. Without pain, how do you know if your faith is for real?

Furthermore, do not wear any self-imposed suffering as a badge of honor. Asceticism (severe self-discipline) is not a substitute for your relationship with Christ, but it can be an enhancer. For example, use the pain and discomfort of fasting to foster your faith in God by bending your will toward His.

Any pain is meant to be a teacher that leads you to look outside yourself for peace and provision in your Savior. However painful it might be to let go of complaining, do it out of obedience and love for Jesus. Productive pain finds peace in God.

How can I remain obedient to God and productive for Him in the middle of my pain?

Praise While in Pain

About midnight Paul and Silas were praying
and singing hymns to God, and the other
prisoners were listening to them.

Acts 16:25

As I recovered from cancer treatment a few years ago, I found the physical discomfort to be excruciating. I asked my wife, Rita, to hold me and play the worship song "How He Loves Us." We sat and embraced each other as we praised and worshiped God. The phrase "My afflictions are eclipsed by His glory" became very real in my painful condition. In the middle of our little worship service, I felt a whole lot of my heavenly Father's love. Praising God in our pain releases His reassuring refrain, "I love you, I love you."

Paul and Silas started the first prison ministry of the New Testament era—from jail! Unscrupulous men with a fortune-telling business were livid after Paul rebuked the evil spirit out of their fortune-teller. These evil men accused the Christian leaders of promoting customs unlawful to Romans and persuaded the government authorities to publicly flog and imprison them. Yet in the middle of Paul and Silas's confinement, they praised Christ Jesus!

But as for me, afflicted and in pain—
may your salvation, God, protect me.

I will praise God's name in song
and glorify him with thanksgiving
(Psalm 69:29-30).

God's grace gives us the ability to praise and thank Him in the middle of our most severe afflictions. Our praise perspective sees and receives the Lord's love above our adversity. We may have encountered unjust treatment, but we know the Just One is in control. Our Savior, Jesus, who allows us to be confined, is the same Savior who sends an earthquake—although not a literal one like that surrounding Paul and Silas's prison—to set us free. When we praise the Lord in our pain, we gain His peace. Hymns sung to God draw us closer to Him.

Perhaps you suffer from rejection, loneliness, financial stress, guilt over the past, fear of the future, chronic caregiving, marital strife, or the pain of a prodigal child or a friend who let you down. Ask the Lord to help you be emboldened, not embittered, in your faith as you journey with Jesus through trials. God inhabits the praises of His people (Psalm 22:3 KJV). Praise God in your pain, and you will bring glory to Him.

The LORD is my strength and my shield;
my heart trusts in him, and he helps me.
My heart leaps for joy,
and with my song I praise him (Psalm 28:7).

Gladness and Sadness

Be glad, people of Zion,
rejoice in the LORD your God,
for he has given you
the autumn rains because he is faithful.
He sends you abundant showers,
both autumn and spring rains, as before.

Joel 2:23

The follower of Jesus cannot remain sad. Yes, you will have seasons of sadness, but you are not meant to stay there as you walk with your Savior through gloomy times. Instead, be grateful to God for little things, like rain, the warmth of the sun, and the cool of the night. God Almighty is the Author of everything, and He is forever providing good things for His children and the opportunity to share all our gifts from God. His blessings elicit smiles on the faces of His children.

Emotional pain may emerge often, your physical pain may be perpetual, and financial pain could be flirting with your peace of mind. Relational pain may be assaulting you with rejection. Pain is a part of life, but do not allow it to pin you to the mat of victimized living. Pain will try to steal your gladness and replace it with sadness. It will show up on your face as a scowl or a jutting jaw. Allow the calm of Christ to caress your countenance; trust Him to bring glad tidings.

He will yet fill your mouth with laughter
and your lips with shouts of joy (Job 8:21).

This is why we worship God in place of the things of this world. Anything outside of the Lord has the potential to let you down. Money will fall short and even contribute to sadness. Children can break your heart, and your spouse will make you sad. Friends will fail you, and circumstances can crush your motivation to care. But abandoning yourself to the Almighty grows faith and a glad face. You cannot remain sad if you are fully abandoned to Him.

Unconditional surrender to your Savior elicits gladness, and a triumphal spirit comes from being in Christ. Peace and contentment are first cousins and the fruit of a glad attitude. Anybody can live a chronically sad life, but those who look to their Savior, Jesus, cannot help but be glad. Be glad for the grace of God that gushes from heaven like a generous geyser. See gladness as a result of resting in the presence of God and engaging with a community of Christ-followers.

Gladness grows in a heart overflowing with gratitude for God's grace and all His good gifts.

[The Lord] satisfies your desires with good things
so that your youth is renewed like the eagle's (Psalm 103:5).

> What sad situation do I need to give over to God so I can become glad in Him?

Joy's Birth Pains

Very truly I tell you, you will weep and mourn while the
world rejoices. You will grieve, but your grief will turn to joy.

John 16:20

Sorrow sometimes lies pregnant in the womb of my soul, waiting to be birthed into joy. I recently wept with a friend whose physical pain brought tears to both our eyes. It hurt me to see him hurt. Joy came as we together sought the comfort of Christ in prayer. I lost my dad years ago when my parents divorced. My joy evaporated and left behind the residue of rage. Thankfully, my anger was converted to love by caring mentors. I experienced God's love through His children. It's when I honestly express my sorrows that my Savior, Jesus, transforms my pain into His peace.

Jesus prepared His disciples for the reality of grief—followed by His guarantee of joy. Jesus was going away, but He promised His followers they would see Him again. What a comfort to know the eyes of the Lord are fixed on those He loves. The disciples would feel the pain of loss, but they could anticipate with joy Christ's return. The deep sorrow experienced at the foot of the cross could be surpassed only by the height of joy standing at the empty tomb. Death brings sorrow, but life brings joy. We can smile and rejoice: Our suffering servant has become our living Lord!

They will come and shout for joy on the heights of Zion…
They will be like a well-watered garden,
and they will sorrow no more (Jeremiah 31:12).

What grief of yours needs a conversion to joy? You feel grief over a death, but you pray the Lord will bring joy back to your life. You feel pain over a prodigal child, but you pray for the return of joy to your heart—even if they don't return. You feel disappointed over unmet expectations, but you leave your desires in God's hands. You feel regret over a ruptured relationship, but you seek the Lord's wisdom for relational repair and joy following repentance.

We go to God in our grief, with anticipation of engaging His deep, abiding joy. Just as the extended roots of a 100-year-old live oak provide stability in the middle of gale-force winds, so the deepening roots of our trust in God stabilize our souls. External circumstances can whip us around and threaten our joy, but the inner peace of Christ abides. Our iceberg of pain begins to melt as it drifts down the warm river of the Lord's love. Rejoicing will follow our mourning.

Weeping may stay for the night,
but rejoicing comes in the morning (Psalm 30:5).

> What pain in my life can Jesus birth into joyful purpose as I rest in Him?

Hurting Spouse

If one part suffers, every part suffers with it; if one part
is honored, every part rejoices with it. Now you are the
body of Christ, and each one of you is a part of it.

1 Corinthians 12:26-27

Sometimes our spouses experience hurt—for a moment; for days, weeks, or months; or in some chronic situations, for years. That hurt can come from a variety of sources: childhood hurt, disappointments, lack of control, shattered dreams, or health issues. Hurt may linger on the surface of your spouse's heart or have inflicted deep wounds. Sadly, the scars of hurt can disfigure your spouse's countenance. Your insensitivity can compound the hurt, or your sensitivity can cure the hurt.

When your spouse hurts, you hurt. You may hurt because of the empathy you feel for her pain. You may hurt because of the pain he has knowingly or unknowingly imposed on you. Hurt cannot be ignored because it will expose itself mildly in public and wildly in private. Hurt will not go away without healing. Your tender touch brings healing. Your extra patience eases the pain. Your kind words are an ointment that soothes anxiety. Your gracious attitude is a legion of love ready to recapture your spouse's heart.

Don't give up reaching out to your hurting spouse.

*Let us not become weary in doing good, for
at the proper time we will reap a harvest
if we do not give up (Galatians 6:9).*

If you are the one who is hurting, go to your heavenly Father for healing. Let Him love you through this. Lay down your burden before it crushes your spirit. You cannot bear this burden by yourself or fix this alone. Your loving Lord wants to lead you into forgiveness and freedom. Release your regret and disappointment to Him; let go of your need for control. Demands for control are the fruit of fear. Remember that Jesus can be trusted during this time of turmoil.

Don't buy into a false feeling of freedom that comes from pushing back. Instead, open up and let the Lord and His love into your heart. Healing is the outcome of applying the outrageous love and forgiveness of God. You may be in a midlife reflection. You are tempted to walk away from your family, friends, and faith, but that is a long and lonely walk that only intensifies the pain.

Take Jesus's advice; go to Him for rest in your weariness and for wholeness for your heart.

*Come to me, all you who are weary and burdened,
and I will give you rest (Matthew 11:28).*

How can I become a safe environment for my spouse to share shame, pain, and sin?

Grief Process

In all this you greatly rejoice, though now for a
little while you may have had to suffer grief in all
kinds of trials. These have come so that the proven
genuineness of your faith...may result in praise,
glory and honor when Jesus Christ is revealed.

1 Peter 1:6-7

Grief is a real source of suffering. We grieve when we lose
a loved one who has gone to be with the Lord. The
memory of the little things we shared in life could linger
with us until the day we go to be with them in glory. We
also grieve when we lose a child to foolish flings. We watch
with broken hearts, unable to control the harmful decisions an adult son or daughter makes, yet we must resist
the temptation to get sucked into the crazy cycle of being
controlled by another person's bad behavior. We temporar-
ily grieve their immature actions, but then we leave them
with God.

We can suffer grief from all kinds of trials that create
troubles—these are tests to refine our faith and lead us to
praise God. Suffering grief and/or trouble can be a tool for
the Spirit to wean us from the world's way of thinking. If
anything other than Christ controls our peace of mind, it is
a threat to our trust in God. The Lord's plan is for us to suffer grief for a "little while."

Our light and momentary troubles are
achieving for us an eternal glory that far
outweighs them all (2 Corinthians 4:17).

Perpetual grieving is not the heart of God for His children. His desire is for praise and rejoicing to follow our faith's refinement. However, during this interim of intense pain, He grieves with us as we process our hurts. His compassionate Spirit draws us into sweeter communion as we enter into a deeper and fuller understanding of our heavenly Father's love and grace. We suffer grief to gain God and to lose ourselves. Grief makes real the precious promises of God.

Most of all, lean into the Lord's longsuffering and unconditional love as you grieve. Get to know your special friend, Jesus, at a new level. Enjoy solitude for a season, but avoid the trap of prolonged isolation. Engage with individuals and a care group who can grieve with you. Grief is not meant to be experienced alone. Processed pain is productive, but unprocessed pain is destructive.

You, God, see the trouble of the afflicted;
you consider their grief and take it in hand.
The victims commit themselves to you (Psalm 10:14).

Who can help me process my pain in a productive fashion?

Patient in Affliction

Be...patient in affliction.

Romans 12:12

Affliction can draw us closer to Christ or drive us away from Christ. It can be a tool of the Lord to build our trust in Him or be a wrecking ball to belief in His goodness. Whether we suffer a heavy or light malady, we accept disruptions as either a blessing or a curse. Sometimes pain is produced in circumstances totally out of our control; other times our unwise decisions create agonizing consequences. Either way, God uses our afflictions for His glory and brings us sweet comfort.

Those who fight against affliction exhaust their energy, but those who embrace difficulties endure. To embrace difficulty does not mean we like pain or enjoy suffering, but it does mean we trust God to work out a good outcome for His glory. He is full of mercy and compassion in the middle of physical upheaval and emotional exhaustion. Thus, we are patient to pray for God's grace to give us the will to wait on Him and to rest in Him. Prayer perseveres.

We count as blessed those who have persevered. You have heard of Job's perseverance and have seen what the Lord finally brought about. The Lord is full of compassion and mercy (James 5:11).

What are you facing that has you focused on your heavenly Father? If disease, make the most of conventional medicine and natural remedies, but mostly go to the Great Physician, Jesus, for care, comfort, and healing. If divorce, lean into the Lord for Him to reconcile you to Himself and for you to be reconciled to severed relationships. If death of a dream or a dear one, pause to grieve and get to know yourself and God at a deeper level. Hard times require a mature patience.

Above all, follow in the steps of Jesus and imitate how He dealt with detrimental circumstances. He wept, yes, but He resolved, "Thy will be done," not "My will be done." He cried out in the night, but eventually He experienced the daybreak of His resurrection. In His most intense time of pain, He forgave ignorant acts and invited a repentant sinner to be with Him in paradise. Jesus was patient in affliction so He could save us and offer us a remedy for our pain—His enduring grace!

Consider him who endured such opposition
from sinners, so that you will not grow
weary and lose heart (Hebrews 12:3).

How can I grow my patience in affliction so I can be a blessing to those around me?

Healing Hurt

Confess your sins to each other and pray for each
other so that you may be healed. The prayer of a
righteous person is powerful and effective.

James 5:16

Hurt cannot be avoided this side of heaven. This is an
unfortunate outcome from outside forces, including self-absorbed family members and insensitive friends,
as well as self-inflicted wounds. The deepest harm comes
from those who should love well, but because of their
own unresolved hurt, they are emotionally injurious.
For example, instead of spouses loving and respecting
their partners, they tear them down with cutting words.
They may withhold affection, tempting their marriage
partner to find affection elsewhere. Sarcasm scars, rejection injures, anger crushes confidence, and dishonesty
destroys trust.

How do we handle deep hurts that have compounded
in crazy cycles over many years? Where do we go when the
hurt is so unbearable that we stay scared, implode in anger,
and grow a root of bitterness? Fortunately, there is hope for
healing in our loving heavenly Father and His caring children. Healing doesn't happen by accident, but begins with
an intentional acknowledgment of the need for wholeness
that can only come by God's grace.

Gracious words are a honeycomb,
sweet to the soul and healing to the bones
(Proverbs 16:24).

By faith in Jesus Christ as your Lord and Savior, you are a precious child of God. He died for you. You are loved by the Lord and by His loving disciples. Confess to Christ your desperate need for His love and forgiveness. Linger long in the accepting arms of Jesus and let Him love you. You are not alone. He was rejected so you could be accepted. He served so you could serve and be served. He died so you could live. His grace heals.

Furthermore, listen to the gracious words of others who love the Lord. What they say is sincere and true. Reject the lies of the Devil and his followers, but embrace the healing truth of trusted friends and counselors. Emotions can betray, but truth keeps you from straying. Confess your sins to Christ and a few confidants, and forgive those who have brought you shameful hurt. Like healing for a deep wound to the flesh, emotional healing takes time. The pain does not go away immediately, and the scab is messy, but the scar is a badge of God's grace.

Then your light will break forth like the dawn,
and your healing will quickly appear;
then your righteousness will go before you,
and the glory of the LORD will be
your rear guard (Isaiah 58:8).

Relational Repair

"Lord," he said, "my servant lies at home paralyzed, suffering
terribly." Jesus said to him, "Shall I come and heal him?"

Matthew 8:6-7

I am learning that relationships are like cars—from time to time they break down. If I ignore the regular maintenance necessary for relationships, it will be to my peril. Marriage, parenting, work, family, and friends all require ongoing evaluation and consistent investment of time and energy. It is especially necessary for me to prayerfully look for ways to serve those whom I have hurt or who have hurt me. Relational repair doesn't mean a perfect relationship, but one that applies love to the wound.

Jesus illustrates this beautifully in His response to the request of a man most despised by the Jewish people. This Roman soldier, who had inflicted pain and suffering on Christ's contemporaries, asked Jesus to heal one of his prized slaves. This powerful centurion unapologetically asked a favor from one who represented a people persecuted by this leader and his government. Jesus chose healing over hate. The Lord served the enemy to grow his faith.

If you are offering your gift at the altar and there
remember that your brother or sister has something
against you, leave your gift there in front of the

> *altar. First go and be reconciled to them; then*
> *come and offer your gift (Matthew 5:23-24).*

Do you need to restore a relationship with someone you may have hurt? Humility and unselfish service go a long way in getting you back in sync with a distant relationship. Go to the offended person and offer help, or go to the one who offended you and offer to serve them. Make restitution in a way that moves the hurt soul toward healing and forgiveness. You can't change the past, but you can love and serve in the present. Relational repair requires an ongoing conversation to restore trust and intimacy.

Most of all, we are wise to keep a healthy relationship with our heavenly Father. Our own unconfessed sins can create a chasm between us and Christ. Sin is subtle as it hijacks our intimacy with the Almighty and replaces it with our own idols. Or in the middle of trials and temptations, we can forget to trust the Lord and distance ourselves from the very thing we need most—God's grace.

Confession and repentance position us for relational healing with our heavenly Father. He reciprocates with love, forgiveness, and reconciliation with Him!

> *Be kind and compassionate to one another,*
> *forgiving each other, just as in Christ God*
> *forgave you (Ephesians 4:32).*

Ask for God's Help on Behalf of the Hurting

When Jesus had entered Capernaum, a
centurion came to him, asking for help.

Matthew 8:5

Do you offer help, or does fear keep you from it? Who in your network of relationships needs your intervention and intercession? Perhaps someone is in financial straits, and you are in a position to give them an anonymous gift or introduce them to a job opportunity. The hurting live all around us. They need help.

> *I think it is necessary to send back to you
> Epaphroditus, my brother, co-worker and fellow
> soldier, who is also your messenger, whom you sent
> to take care of my needs (Philippians 2:25).*

Be bold in your requests for those who do not have a platform for their pain. Maybe this means you stand in the gap for people devastated by a natural disaster. You can serve them in the power of Jesus, with the compassion of Jesus, for the gospel of Jesus. You know Jesus is their greatest source of strength and forgiveness, so do not be stingy with His grace and with good deeds. The needy need Christians who care with words and works.

*I looked for someone among them who would
build up the wall and stand before me in the
gap on behalf of the land so I would not have to
destroy it, but I found no one (Ezekiel 22:30).*

You can solicit your Savior to heal the hurting and save their souls. Your heavenly Father listens and responds to an affectionate appeal from His children. When you address the Lord in prayer on behalf of those who struggle in sin and sickness, you make a difference. Your heartfelt petitions engage eternal resources that come to their rescue. So stay faithful in asking heaven to help with matters on earth. He cares to cure!

Whom do you know who need the Lord's help? Have you, on bended knee, petitioned Jesus on their behalf? Be bold for their sakes and for the glory of God. Go to Jesus so someone can get to Jesus for healing and forgiveness. It takes time to be an advocate for another, but your valuable time is a gift from God. Steward it well by seeking each day to serve your colleagues, friends, family, enemies, and strangers. Your Master gives you margin in your calendar not for the frivolous, but for faith issues. Leverage your possessions and gifts for your Savior, Jesus, so others can be blessed.

Because we know Him, we can make Him known by asking Him to heal the hurting.

*The LORD heard Hezekiah and healed
the people (2 Chronicles 30:20).*

On whose behalf do I need to intercede with the Lord? For whom do I need to be an advocate?

Seek the Lord's Help for Yourself

The woman came and knelt before
him. "Lord, help me!" she said.

Matthew 15:25

A life lived well requires help from the Lord. Life is like a ship on the open sea: We navigate through calm waters, rough waters, uncertain waters, and beautiful waters—but all the time trusting the Captain. The source of our strength must be Christ, or we grow chronically tired. Faith in the Lord triumphs over fear and frustration.

God's help is provided to those who kneel in humble dependency and cry out to Jesus, "Lord, help me!" When our body writhes in pain, we cry for help. When a critical word crushes our spirit, we cry for help. When unanswered questions stalk our minds, we cry for help. When relational conflict emaciates our emotions, we cry for help. Help from heaven gives hope, healing, and the energy to push through tough times and trust Him.

The LORD is my strength and my shield;
my heart trusts in him, and he helps me.

My heart leaps for joy,
and with my song I praise him (Psalm 28:7).

His help gives joy where laughter has left. His help gives confidence in the middle of crisis. His help forgives when hurt has severed another's trust. His help harnesses grace and bridles a toxic tongue. His help reaches to the poorest of the poor, the richest of the rich, and everyone in between with His saving grace in Jesus Christ. His help helps.

How can Jesus help you? Do you need wisdom? Ask Him with a humble heart, and He will hear and answer your request. His response may come in the form of godly friends who give you wise advice. Look around and listen intently, for the Lord speaks through those who truly love you. Jesus helps those who humbly seek out and trust wise counsel.

When a mocker is punished, the simple gain wisdom;
by paying attention to the wise they
get knowledge (Proverbs 21:11).

What help do I need from the Lord?

Overcoming Relational Barriers

When a Samaritan woman came to draw water, Jesus said
to her, "Will you give me a drink?"…The woman said,
"I know that Messiah" (called Christ) "is coming. When
he comes, he will explain everything to us." Then Jesus
declared, "I, the one speaking to you—I am he."

John 4:7,25-26

Jesus was thirsty for water, but He was also thirsty for this woman to learn of Him—God's living water. He dismissed the barriers of cultural bias and went right to her heart. Although women of His day were treated with contempt, Jesus related to her with compassion. And despite the prevalent racial prejudice of the times, He listened intently to her ideas about God. Yes, overcoming relational barriers starts by being respectful to the person with opposing ideas, no matter your differences.

Built-in cultural divides exist when diverse people come together to communicate. Family traditions, religious beliefs, regional pride, racial judgments, social status, and preconceived notions are a few. However, the unconditional acceptance and love of Christ cuts through cultural clutter and creates a clear path of communication and understanding. We create trust when we seek to understand the other person's paradigms and are humbly bold about our own beliefs.

*Jews and Gentiles alike are all under
the power of sin (Romans 3:9).*

The entire human race began from the same place. No one people group is superior, but all are subject to the one and only King Jesus. So it's with caring concern that we approach individuals different in origin and opinion. Outside of Christ, we are all sinners in need of a Savior. In Christ, we are all sinners saved by grace. Thus, we prayerfully seek common ground. The gospel of Jesus Christ assimilates diverse backgrounds.

Where is the Lord calling you to build relational bridges? A neighbor not native to your area or a professional acquaintance who professes unbelief in God? Humans hunger for answers to life, and God has placed in everyone's heart a thirst for Him. We who are refreshed by Christ's living water are called to educate thirsty souls in how they can be satisfied. Be creative and use everyday experiences to engage in spiritual conversation. Explain how your once-parched heart has been hydrated by the living water of Jesus.

Yes, Christ overcomes relational barriers!

*God does not show favoritism but accepts from
every nation the one who fears him and does what is
right. You know the message God sent to the people
of Israel, announcing the good news of peace through
Jesus Christ, who is Lord of all (Acts 10:34-36).*

> How can I be intentional to understand those who
> are different from me with the goal of sharing Jesus?

Gain from Loss

Whatever were gains to me I now consider loss for the
sake of Christ. What is more, I consider everything a
loss because of the surpassing worth of knowing Christ
Jesus my Lord, for whose sake I have lost all things.
I consider them garbage, that I may gain Christ.

Philippians 3:7-8

In God's economy, some of our greatest gains come with
losses. We lose a son or daughter to marriage, but we gain
a daughter-in-law or son-in-law. We lose a corporate job,
but we gain an opportunity to influence a smaller enter-
prise for God's kingdom. We lose our health, but we gain
a realization of the brevity of life, becoming more intentional in matters of faith and eternity. We lose an opportunity because we lacked peace, but we gain an opportunity
that excites our imagination.

What have you lost that needs repair or replacement?
If it's your reputation, lean into the Lord to restore your
character in the community. As you walk with Christ in
integrity, you will gain a good name that is many times more

valuable than gold. Maybe you made a hard decision that caused you to lose a long-term relationship. Yet you may have gained their respect, and one day they may truly desire to know you at a deeper emotional level. God's gains far exceed our losses.

Whoever rebukes a person will in the end gain favor
rather than one who has a flattering
tongue (Proverbs 28:23).

The surpassing worth of knowing Christ Jesus as Lord is our greatest gain. We clamor to see popes, pastors, and presidents, while all the while the King of Kings and Lord of Lords kindly waits to love us. No need for us to gain access to God; He has given us the full privilege of being with Him and knowing Him—anytime, anywhere. We need no Secret Service agents to overcome because the blood of our Savior, Jesus, has already overcome! By faith we gain God.

Whatever things we give up to gain God are mere trinkets in His kingdom. We give up the trinket of distrust and gain our Lord's diamond ring of trust. We give up the trinket of striving and gain our Savior's safety-deposit box filled with His peace and security. We give up the trinket of people's approval and gain our heavenly Father's warm acceptance and compassionate understanding. The exchange rate of our culture's currency offers us losses, but Christ's currency gives us gains.

Those who have served well gain an excellent
standing and great assurance in their faith
in Christ Jesus (1 Timothy 3:13).

How God Defines Greatness

He will be great in the sight of the Lord.

Luke 1:15

What does it mean to be great to God? Obtaining riches, possibly. But humility and a servant spirit? Absolutely! A CEO or a general in the military? These leaders could be great, but power does not guarantee greatness; in many cases, it tempts true greatness. God's estimation of greatness is the courage to do the right thing as He defines right—like John the Baptist, to whom Luke 1:15 refers, did. Jesus said he was like a reed unshaken by the wind (Luke 7:24). Greatness means standing faithfully with God without wavering.

Greatness to God means we give up our job if it means giving in to ethical compromise. Greatness assumes I am willing to offend a friend if their expectation of me offends my heavenly Father. True greatness gladly becomes the servant of all and does not expect to be served at all. God measures greatness by what we give, not by what we accumulate. Indeed, generosity is godly greatness. We are the greatest when we are rich toward God.

*Whoever wants to become great among you
must be your servant (Matthew 20:26).*

Your great love for your great God will cause you to take a stand for His great ideas. Godly people pursue God, and in the process they capture greatness. Your influence expands exponentially when you are defined by eternity's agenda. Sharing the gospel, discipling others, feeding the working poor, caring for the mentally and physically challenged, adopting orphans, serving widows, granting unconditional love, and offering forgiveness are all great to God.

However, hold these great truths with a sober mind and a humble heart. Few are won over and kept by laser-like logic and passionate persuasiveness. The Spirit will draw people to Jesus by your grace and love. In a spirit of sensitivity and prayer, lay out your rational faith at the right time. The world's stage gives its great actors loud accolades, but in your greatest moment of truth, listen only for the Lord's quiet applause. Imitate Jesus, who is the greatest!

*God exalted him to the highest place and gave him
the name that is above every name, that at the
name of Jesus every knee should bow, in heaven
and on earth and under the earth, and every tongue
acknowledge that Jesus Christ is Lord, to the
glory of God the Father (Philippians 2:9-11).*

Gratitude Draws Us to God

I, with shouts of grateful praise,
will sacrifice to you.
What I have vowed I will make good.
I will say, "Salvation comes from the LORD."

Jonah 2:9

My gratitude draws me to God in grateful praise. My worshipful heart wanders into the land of thankfulness and settles my soul on the homestead of the Lord's wonder. My imagination expands into creative thinking when I am thankful to Jesus for His everlasting salvation. His Spirit shows me possibilities that ungratefulness cannot comprehend. Gratitude leads me to the Lord. The end goal of my thankful soul is to rest in the Shepherd of my soul.

Jonah struggled to have a grateful heart toward God. He did not want to leave his comfort zone and disturb the comfort of Nineveh's naysayers. The Lord took Jonah through a gauntlet of adversity to develop within him a heart of gratitude to God. In his darkest moment, he released his worthless idols of fear and selfishness and embraced grateful praise and sacrifice to the Almighty. Once Jonah acknowledged the Lord as his salvation, he was delivered into the light. He made good on his vow to do good. His gratitude intersected with God's grace.

*All this is for your benefit, so that the grace
that is reaching more and more people
may cause thanksgiving to overflow to the
glory of God (2 Corinthians 4:15).*

Do you direct your gratitude to God first? Someone might say to a spouse, "I thank God for bringing you into my life." A friend might acknowledge another friend as a gift from the Lord. Thank your heavenly Father first, and He is sure to get the glory of your gratitude. Gratitude praises God for what we have, and trusts God for what we do not have.

Almighty God is the Creator of our complex creation, and so we are simultaneously grateful for both the major blessings in life—family, freedom, friends, and health—and the daily delights—a sunrise, a sunset, rest, a good meal, a smile, and the coo of an infant. Gratitude is hopeful, helpful, gracious, generous, and worshipful.

Let's bow our heads and thank the Lord for our abundant life in Christ.

*We also thank God continually because, when you
received the word of God, which you heard from
us, you accepted it not as a human word, but as
it actually is, the word of God, which is indeed at
work in you who believe (1 Thessalonians 2:13).*

Sickness for God's Glory

Jesus said, "This sickness will not end in death. No, it is for
God's glory so that God's Son may be glorified through it."

John 11:4

Sickness is an opportunity for God to be glorified and for
observers to believe in Jesus, God's Son. This perspective is easy to forget because sickness is often a struggle. The
physical body can be extremely demanding. It can writhe
in pain, convulse from seizures, sweat from fever, ache from
infection, and fatigue from cancer. Some feel so bad they are
ready to go home to heaven. In the meantime, illness can be
a hard yet meaningful experience for God's glory.

The Lord uses sickness to draw people to one another
and to Himself. A sick child causes Mom and Dad to come
together on their knees on behalf of their precious one.
Elderly parents who are ill are an invitation for adult children to spend time together and to work together for the
betterment of their parents' quality of life. As we serve the
sick, those who need Jesus see His love in action.

*The strong spirit of a man sustains him
in bodily pain or trouble, but a weak
and broken spirit who can raise up or
bear? (Proverbs 18:14 AMPC).*

Are you struggling with sickness? If so, seek to experience the intimacy of God's glory in the middle of your illness. Your afflictions can be eclipsed by His glory. Similar to the stamina of a parent caring for a needy child, His glory engulfs your soul with energy to endure chronic pain. The sweet spot of His Spirit provides security in your sickness. Christ's peace guards your heart and mind to get through intense health issues, and God's glory gives you hope and healing.

Is someone you love suffering from an illness? How can you glorify God in your love for them? Start with a simple prayer for the Holy Spirit to strengthen your sick family member or friend by His grace and love. Quietly listen. Share Scripture with them, such as Psalm 59:16-17, for comfort and peace. Your faith in God is a rock to those whose world is being shaken by adversity. Be available to support them by caring for their children or raising funds to pay for their medical bills.

Boldly share Jesus with the sick in love and with humility.

In your hearts revere Christ as Lord.
Always be prepared to give an answer to
everyone who asks you to give the reason for the
hope that you have. But do this with gentleness
and respect (1 Peter 3:15).

Hurried Sickness

Come with me by yourselves to a quiet place and get some rest.

Mark 6:31

Hurried sickness is more than being busy; it is an unhealthy pace of living. We wake up one day and find ourselves overcommitted and underresourced. Spiritually, we are unavailable for God. In our routine, we may rush through a religious service, but our heart is not engaged with the heart of Jesus. Mentally, we are overly stimulated by too many shiny things. Computers, mobile devices, and media all insist we be available on demand. Hurried sickness leaves only a shell of a soul.

Jesus recognized His disciples had crossed over the line when He noticed they were too busy to eat. Their works for God had replaced their time with God. They had to courageously tell people no for a period of time so they could tell their heavenly Father yes. A mind without rest can become restless, discontent, and in danger of making unwise decisions. Selfish taking, self-reliance, and self-pity can drive our feelings when we find ourselves emotionally frazzled. Jesus knew that without rest His disciples were also more vulnerable to the prideful effects of success.

You may say to yourself, "My power and the strength of my hands have produced this wealth for me."

*But remember the LORD your God, for it is he who gives
you the ability to produce wealth (Deuteronomy 8:17-18).*

Do you see symptoms of hurried sickness in your life? Impatience, anger, fear, double booking, not returning phone calls or e-mails in a timely fashion, or being late for appointments may call for a boycott of busyness. Perhaps your child can participate in only one (or no) extracurricular activity outside of regular school hours so your family can rest and reconnect with God. Maybe it's time to hire an administrative assistant who can protect your calendar from a frantic pace. Hurried sickness is the natural progression of a busy culture, so we must prayerfully adjust.

Find a quiet place and rest. Make Sunday an authentic day of renewal and worship. Doing nothing is doing a lot! Rest gives us the resolve to stand up to injustice and the humility to sit down and listen. Rest opens vistas of creativity to our minds and closes doors on unseemly influences. Rest is a relational lubricant and a physical recharge. Above all, rest brings peace to our souls. It feeds our spirits and grows our faith. We hear the Lord more clearly when it's quiet. Rest is God's gift to carry on in His strength.

Yes, the remedy to hurried sickness is quiet rest with Jesus.

*Be still before the LORD and wait
patiently for him (Psalm 37:7).*

How to Become a Disciple of Jesus Christ

Then Jesus came to them and said, "All authority
in heaven and on earth has been given to me.
Therefore go and make disciples of all nations,
baptizing them in the name of the Father and of the
Son and of the Holy Spirit, and teaching them to
obey everything I have commanded you. And surely
I am with you always, to the very end of the age."

Matthew 28:18-20

Holy Scripture teaches us how to become disciples and how to make disciples.

Believe

Belief in Jesus Christ as your Savior and Lord gives you eternal life in heaven.

If you declare with your mouth, "Jesus is Lord," and
believe in your heart that God raised him from
the dead, you will be saved (Romans 10:9).

Repent and Be Baptized

To repent is to turn from your sin and then publicly confess Christ in baptism.

*Repent and be baptized, every one of you, in
the name of Jesus Christ for the forgiveness
of your sins. And you will receive the gift
of the Holy Spirit (Acts 2:38).*

Obey

Obedience is an indicator of our love for the Lord Jesus and
His presence in our life.

*Jesus replied, "Anyone who loves me will obey my
teaching. My Father will love them, and we will come
to them and make our home with them" (John 14:23).*

Worship, Prayer, Community, Evangelism, and Study

Worship and prayer express our gratitude and honor to God
and our dependence on His grace. Community and evan-
gelism show our accountability to Christians and compassion for non-Christians. We study to apply the knowledge,
understanding, and wisdom of God.

*Every day they continued to meet together in the
temple courts. They broke bread in their homes
and ate together with glad and sincere hearts,
praising God and enjoying the favor of all the
people. And the Lord added to their number daily
those who were being saved (Acts 2:46-47).*

Love God

Intimacy with Almighty God is a growing and loving relationship. We are loved by Him, so we can love others and be empowered by the Holy Spirit to obey His commands.

> *Jesus replied: "'Love the Lord your God with all your heart and with all your soul and with all your mind.' This is the first and greatest commandment" (Matthew 22:37-38).*

Love People

Our love for others flows from our love for our heavenly Father. We can love because He first loved us.

> *And the second is like it: "Love your neighbor as yourself" (Matthew 22:39).*

Make Disciples

We disciple others because we are grateful to God and to those who disciple us, and we want to obey Christ's last instructions before going to heaven.

> *The things you have heard me say in the presence of many witnesses entrust to reliable people who will also be qualified to teach others (2 Timothy 2:2).*

Where to Find...

Acknowledgments

Thank you, Brother Marcellus, from the Abbey of the Genesee outside of Rochester, New York, for being Jesus to me during a painful time in my life.

Thank you, Wisdom Hunters team, for loving like Jesus: Rita Bailey, Gwynne Maffett, Shanna Schutte, Rachel Snead, Rachel Prince, Tripp Prince, and Susan Fox.

Thank you, Susan Fox and Jean Kavich Bloom, for your expert editing.

Thank you, Wisdom Hunters board of directors, for your love, prayers, and accountability: Cliff Bartow, Andrew Wexler, and John Hightower. Former board members: Deb Ochs and Jack McEntee.

Thank you, National Christian Foundation, for the opportunity, by God's grace, to reach and restore every person by the love of Christ—and to mobilize biblical generosity for God's kingdom.

Thank you, Harvest House Publishers, for your vision and support for this book: Bob Hawkins, Sherrie Slopianka, Shannon Hartley, Gene Skinner, Terry Glaspey, Ken Lorenz, Kathy Zemper, and Brad Moses.

About the Author

Boyd Bailey is the president of the National Christian Foundation (NCF) in Georgia. His passion is to help leaders grow giving hearts so they can experience the joy of generosity.

Since 2004 he has also served as president and founder of Wisdom Hunters, a ministry that connects people to Christ through devotional writing, with more than 125,000 daily e-mail, app, and social media readers.

In 1999 Boyd cofounded Ministry Ventures, which has trained approximately 1000 faith-based nonprofits and coached for certification more than 200 ministries in the best practices of prayer, board development, ministry model, administration, and fundraising. By God's grace, these ministries have raised more than $100 million, and thousands of people have been led into growing relationships with Jesus Christ.

Prior to Ministry Ventures, Boyd was the national director for Crown Financial Ministries. He was instrumental in the expansion of Crown into 30 major markets across the United States. He was a key facilitator in the $25 million merger between Christian Financial Concepts and Crown Ministries.

Before his work with Crown, Boyd and Andy Stanley started First Baptist Atlanta's north campus, and as an elder, Boyd assisted Andy in the start of North Point Community Church.

Boyd received a bachelor of arts degree from Jacksonville State University and a master of divinity degree from Southwestern Seminary in Fort Worth, Texas. Boyd and his wife, Rita, live in Roswell, Georgia. They have been married 39 years and are blessed with four daughters, four sons-in-law, and nine grandchildren.

Rita Bailey is the first follower of Wisdom Hunters and wife to Boyd. In the early days, she served as administrator, book mailer, donor appreciator and encourager. More recently, she has more time to spend traveling and serving with Boyd. She also enjoys time spent with their four adult daughters and families, which include nine precious grandchildren, qualifying her as chief of content inspiration.

Wisdom Hunters

Walk with the wise and become wise, for a
companion of fools suffers harm.

PROVERBS 13:20

In 2004, Boyd Bailey began to informally e-mail personal reflections from his morning devotional time to a select group of fellow wisdom hunters. Over time, these informal e-mails grew into the Wisdom Hunters Daily Devotional. Today these e-mails reach more than 125,000 wisdom hunters each morning.

We remain relentless in the pursuit of wisdom and continue to daily write raw, original, real-time reflections from our personal encounters with the Lord. In addition to our daily e-mails, these writings are available on our blog, Facebook, and Twitter. The thoughtful comments and wisdom our followers share each day can help us all in our journeys with God.

Our past devotionals on marriage, wisdom, wise living, fatherhood, and more are available in book form. Visit us at www.wisdom hunters.com.

The National Christian Foundation

Founded in 1982 and based in Atlanta, Georgia, the National Christian Foundation (NCF) is a charitable giving ministry that provides wise giving solutions, mobilizes resources, and inspires biblical generosity with Christian families, advisers, and charities. NCF is currently the ninth-largest US nonprofit, having accepted more than $9 billion in contributions and granted more than $7 billion to more than 40,000 charities. The NCF Giving Fund, or donor-advised fund, allows donors to make charitable contributions and then recommend grants to the charities they care about over time. NCF is also an industry leader in accepting gifts of appreciated assets, such as stocks, real estate, and business interests, which enables donors to save taxes and align their charitable goals with their family, business, estate, and legacy plans. Learn more about NCF at www.ncfgiving.com.

More Great Harvest House Books by Boyd Bailey

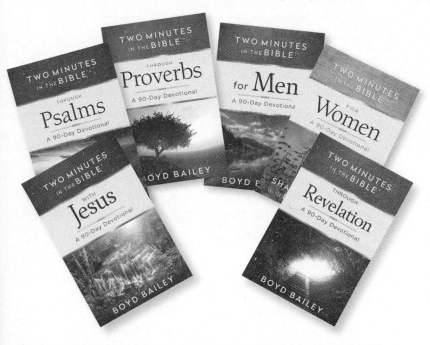

To learn more about Harvest House books
or to read sample chapters, visit our website:
www.HarvestHousePublishers.com